'There are several very good authors in the world of contemporary psychoanalysis who can be placed in the area that we broadly call relational, but despite their originality they can always be reabsorbed into the so-called mainstream. Not so Antonino Ferro. His thinking is revolutionary. No one like him has so thoroughly changed the way we understand the therapeutic relationship and practice psychoanalysis. Always proceeding with courage, consistency, great intelligence and a very human sense of humour, he has helped revitalize a noble art, but one that sometimes runs the risk of being reduced to ritualistic repetition of empty formulas, more the litany of a religious rite than the exercise of a true love for research about the essence of what makes us human. It is about time that a monograph devoted entirely to him and his thought saw the light of day. For this we must be grateful to Robert Snell, the author of this beautiful book. It is easy to predict that it will be a great success among all psychotherapists, psychoanalysts, humanities scholars and educated people interested in psychoanalysis.'

Giuseppe Civitarese, *author of* Sublime Subjects:
Aesthetic Experience and Intersubjectivity
in Psychoanalysis, *2017,*
London, Routledge

'The mastery of Bion's work and familiarity with Italian psychoanalysis make Robert Snell's work a precious manual of post-Bionian Field Theory. The clear style and the competent and balanced attitude make reading pleasant, not only to those who want to approach the fundamentals

T0372850

of BFT but also to those who, already familiar with it, want to bring order to theoretical concepts and clinical practice.'

Fulvio Mazzacane, *Member of the SPI, President of the Centro Psicoanalitico di Pavia*

'I wanted to express my deep appreciation for your remarkable work that I have had the privilege of re-reading. As I absorbed the intricacies of the book, I found myself enthralled by the meticulous precision with which you delved into my thoughts, respecting my words and traversing each conceptual junction with unwavering patience. The profound essence of certain landscapes took on new meaning for me through the pages of this book. I would like to extend my heartfelt gratitude to you for your respect and understanding of the ideas put forth by complex authors. My sincere thanks for your invaluable contribution.'

Antonino Ferro, *President of the Italian Psychoanalytic Society, Training and Supervising Analyst in the Italian Psychoanalytic Society, the American Psychoanalytic Association, and the International Psychoanalytical Association*

Antonino Ferro

This book provides a clear, thorough, and accessible introduction to the work of Antonino Ferro and draws on the clinical vignettes that punctuate his writings to show how Ferro has built on Bion's revolutionary achievements to develop a distinctive, game-changing version of field theory in psychoanalysis.

The book clarifies the phenomenological insight that the analyst and the patient together generate an ever-evolving, intersubjective field. Rather than the supposed psychology of the individual, it is this populous and multidimensional field, a co-created 'in-between' rich in characters and stories, that is to be explored and elaborated. The primary points of access to this new 'multiverse' are dream, reverie, metaphor, and imagination. A radical Negative Capability is called for, not least to help dissolve co-constructed 'bastions' obstructing the field's expansion. The book sketches out the Italian and international context in which Ferro developed his thinking and addresses some key critical questions. It concludes that Ferro's life's work, which marries theoretical rigour with a revitalising increase in playfulness and freedom of response, is a transformational force within psychoanalysis and a major catalyst in its evolution.

This important volume is rewarding reading for beginning and seasoned analysts alike, as well as for psychotherapists, counsellors, humanities scholars, and anyone interested in psychoanalysis.

Robert Snell (Ph.D.) is a psychoanalytic psychotherapist in private practice, a member of the British Psychoanalytic Council and the British Psychotherapy Foundation, and an Honorary Senior Research Fellow at Roehampton University, UK.

Routledge Introductions to Contemporary Psychoanalysis

Aner Govrin, Ph.D.
Series Editor
Yael Peri Herzovich, Ph.D.
Executive Editor
Itamar Ezer
Assistant Editor

'Routledge Introductions to Contemporary Psychoanalysis' is one of the prominent psychoanalytic publishing ventures of our day. It will comprise dozens of books that will serve as concise introductions dedicated to influential concepts, theories, leading figures, and techniques in psychoanalysis covering every important aspect of psychoanalysis.

The length of each book is fixed at 40,000 words.

The series' books are designed to be easily accessible to provide informative answers in various areas of psychoanalytic thought. Each book will provide updated ideas on topics relevant to contemporary psychoanalysis – from the unconscious and dreams, projective identification, and eating disorders, through neuropsychoanalysis, colonialism, and spiritual-sensitive psychoanalysis. Books will also be dedicated to prominent figures in the field, such as Melanie Klein, Jaque Lacan, Sandor Ferenczi, Otto Kernberg, and Michael Eigen.

Not serving solely as an introduction for beginners, the purpose of the series is to offer compendiums of information on particular topics within different psychoanalytic schools. We ask authors to review a topic but also address the readers with their own personal views and contribution to the specific chosen field. Books will make intricate ideas comprehensible without compromising their complexity.

We aim to make contemporary psychoanalysis more accessible to both clinicians and the general educated public.

Aner Govrin – Editor

Marion Milner: A Contemporary Introduction
Alberto Stefana and Alessio Gamba

James F. Masterson: A Contemporary Introduction
Loray Daws

Antonino Ferro: A Contemporary Introduction
Robert Snell

Antonino Ferro

A Contemporary Introduction

Robert Snell

Routledge
Taylor & Francis Group

LONDON AND NEW YORK

Designed cover image: Michal Heiman, Asylum 1855-2020, The Sleeper (video, psychoanalytic sofa and Plate 34), exhibition view, Herzliya Museum of Contemporary Art, 2017

First published 2024
by Routledge
4 Park Square, Milton Park, Abingdon, Oxon OX14 4RN

and by Routledge
605 Third Avenue, New York, NY 10158

Routledge is an imprint of the Taylor & Francis Group, an informa business

British Library Cataloguing-in-Publication Data
A catalogue record for this book is available from the British Library

ISBN: 9781032321974 (hbk)
ISBN: 9781032321967 (pbk)
ISBN: 9781003313311 (ebk)

DOI: 10.4324/9781003313311

Typeset in Times New Roman
by codeMantra

Contents

Figures

Preface and Acknowledgements

The work of Antonino Ferro is ground breaking. It opens up whole new understandings of what might be going on in the analytic encounter. It radically frees up our thinking about how patients and analysts can be together. Building on Bion's revolutionary achievements, Ferro recasts a foundational psychoanalytic principle: for him the unconscious is no longer just, or primarily, a repository of the repressed, but something constantly co-generated. The idea of the analytic space as a co-created, dynamic, evolving inter-personal *field* has enabled tremendous refinements of listening, theory and technique, and expanded the potential of psychoanalysis and psychoanalytic psychotherapy to bring about transformations.

This book aims to be an introduction to an already highly accessible body of work. It is also the first book to explore how Ferro's way of thinking and working has been shaped by historical and geographical circumstance – shaped, but not confined or limited. Seeking to locate his work within its wider context, it also addresses key areas of the critical debate Ferro has generated.

My own introduction to Ferro came about through a reading group set up on the English south coast by Richard Morgan-Jones around 2015. It took me a while, as a practising analytic psychotherapist trained in London, to realise what was on offer: a way of approaching analytic practice and theory that was not only unfamiliar and challenging, but also liberating and reinvigorating.

The thinking of Ferro and his colleague Giuseppe Civitarese was the catalyst for a book in which I explored the idea that Cézanne's painting might illuminate the work of Bion and vice versa (Snell 2021). The manuscript met with enthusiasm from Civitarese and Ferro himself, and this, thanks also to the energetic support of Gillian Jarvis, Ferro's Personal Assistant, led to contact with the lively group of analysts living and working around Ferro in Pavia, Lombardy, and to the publication of a special international 'field' edition, edited by Del Loewenthal, Richard and me, of *The European Journal of Psychotherapy and Counselling* (Snell and Morgan-Jones 2022, and Snell, Morgan-Jones and Loewenthal, 2023).

When Ferro was asked by Aner Govrin and Tair Caspi, the editors of the Routledge Introductions to Contemporary Psychoanalysis series, to suggest someone who might write on his work for the series, he kindly passed on my name. I have since had the great pleasure of visiting Pavia and meeting him, and he has warmly endorsed what follows.

The consulting room, Ferro and Civitarese have written, should be 'an atelier filled with as much creative mess as we are able to tolerate' (Ferro and Civitarese 2015, p. xvi). I hope this book is faithful not just to the conceptual letter but also to the generous spirit of Ferro's work, and that it will encourage readers to join him in the studio/workshop. It might be read in conjunction with Howard Levine's *The Post-Bionian Field Theory of Antonino Ferro* (2022), and with companion volumes in the present series: Giuseppe Civitarese's *Psychoanalytic Field Theory* (2023), Annie Reiner's *W. R. Bion's Theories of Mind* (2023), and Meg Harris Williams's *Donald Meltzer* (2022). Best of all, it might propel the reader towards Ferro's own extensive (and mostly translated) writings and to an enjoyment of their revitalising effect.

I owe a very large debt of gratitude to Richard Morgan-Jones for the friendship and the inspiration, clinical and intellectual, that he has offered me over many years. This book has been greatly enriched and refined by his comments, particularly around embodiment, and links between the field, the group and the organisation.

Very special thanks to Gill Jarvis, whose support and enthusiasm for this project have been utterly invaluable. I thank her too, and the friends and colleagues in Pavia to whom she introduced me, especially Fulvio Mazzacane, Antonino Gallo, Maurizio Collovà, and Giovanni Foresti, for their warm welcome at the Centro Psicoanalitico di Pavia conference in June 2023.

Thank you, Maurizio, for pointing me towards Cézanne's 'Card Players', and Mark Fletcher, Lorraine Gillingham, Frank Gray, Del Loewenthal, Lawrence Suss, and other friends and colleagues in the UK with whom I have shared conversations. I am especially indebted to Howard Levine and Giuseppe Civitarese for their interest and encouragement, and to Claudio Neri who, about a decade ago, first put me in touch with them both. I am sincerely grateful to Aner Govrin and Tair Caspi, and to my editors at Routledge.

I hope Antonino Ferro will accept this book as the best token I can offer of my thanks and esteem.

And the biggest thank you of all is to my wife Kim, for her tremendous patience and good spirits throughout the book's gestation.

Quotations from literary and other non-psychoanalytic sources have been selected by me, unless otherwise acknowledged.

Introduction

Keywords

Thinking thoughts, living emotions, living in the terror we can feel, taking upon ourselves the suffering of others, contacting the creativity in ourselves and in our patients, and letting it emerge, are perhaps good enough reasons for living, albeit in the full awareness of the insignificance of human existence. If, that is, we could accept the claim that we are a whim of nature, as Lucretius said, and if we were aware of the terror that this generates in us (and which is all the greater the more we deny it), then perhaps we might be able to do what the British and German troops did, as Bion reminds us, at the front on Christmas Day: play football in no man's land. If we could play with life's non-sense, maybe to the horror of all the high-ranking fundamentalists, we would open up chinks of understanding and peace.

(Ferro [2014] 2019, p. 100)

What else is it that drives us in our exciting job if not the desire to discover what exists beyond the Pillars of Hercules of the repetition compulsion? What is it in the parallel universes that expects the Starship Enterprise to continue its

DOI: 10.4324/9781003313311-1

journey? Fortunately we don't know the answer! Giving a name to what we do without knowing that we are doing it is, in my opinion, what research in psychoanalysis is about.

(Ferro 2007, p. 176)

In bringing together Bion and theories of the interpersonal field, Antonino Ferro can claim a place as a psychoanalytic pioneer in line of succession from Freud, Klein, Winnicott, and Bion himself. Alongside Donald Meltzer, James Grotstein, and Thomas Ogden, he is undoubtedly among the most creative of Bion's heirs. But are we (to paraphrase Bion) already running the risk of sinking him under a weight of plaudits before we have even left port? In Ferro's case, the risk seems negligible, for his thinking and writing are nothing if not buoyant. His enormous contribution to psychoanalysis might equally be summed up in a couple of words: 'play' and 'vitality'.

Vitalità e gioco in psicoanalisi (*Playing and Vitality in Psychoanalysis*) is the title of a book Ferro published with Giuseppe Civitarese in 2020, and this immediately brings us to another keyword: collaboration. A pioneer does not have to be a solitary genius. Ferro has a central place in a highly creative group of analysts in Pavia, and across the globe, although the position of presiding maestro is not one he would insist upon; Civitarese, for example, has been prolific in elaborating Ferro's thought and its theoretical underpinnings. That psychoanalysis is a living collaboration, between colleagues but above all between analyst and patient, is at the heart of Ferro's way of thinking and working. It is collaboration in a potentially life-giving form of play – a serious game, to be played with humour and respect.

He has often written in partnership, and it is sometimes difficult to say whose contribution is whose. And now we make contact with another key concept: that of the intersubjective, transpersonal 'field', in which it is hard to distinguish one partner's contribution from the other's. The metaphor of the 'field' is central to Ferro's work: the idea that from the moment patient and analyst get together, they co-create something new and unknown, an unfolding dynamic, emotional field, something more than the sum of their individual contributions. In his development of the concept, Ferro has vastly extended our appreciation of the phenomenology of the analytic encounter.[1]

The 'field' idea might be illustrated by one of Cézanne's paintings of card players. Two figures in an interior, closely framed in a shallow space, are absorbed in a game. Each maintains his individuality, but they share both the game and a palpable atmosphere made of the same stuff – a patterning of coloured brushstrokes – as themselves. 'The mere fact of being in a room already modifies the chemical composition of the air breathed by its occupants' (Ferro and Civitarese 2015, p. 9).

Like dancers in a dance, the players are absorbed in the game. Ferro and Civitarese's *Playing and Vitality in Psychoanalysis* is a gathering of writings – papers, adapted book chapters – from previous publications which, it struck the authors, now seemed to coalesce around a theme in a way that had not been so apparent before. This too is characteristic of an approach to working, thinking, and imagining. Ideas, insights, and intuitions offer themselves to be seen from new angles, so that they come

Figure 1 Paul Cézanne, *Card Players*, between 1890 and 1895, oil on canvas, 47.5×56.5cm. Paris, Musée d'Orsay. Legacy of comte Isaac de Camondo, 1911. Photo RMN-Grand Palais (Musée d'Orsay) / Patrice Schmidt. Public Domain

together in sometimes surprising ways and generate new ideas. Ferro's way of thinking and writing is of a piece with his practice and philosophy of psychoanalysis.

At this point, the reader may be hearing echoes from across the wider psychoanalytic field. For Ferro's work is a sustained conversation with forbears as well as contemporaries, and with British forbears in particular: with Winnicott, who gave such primacy to play and its connection to aliveness, and in the 'Squiggle' game gave us a vivid example of an interpersonal field in action; and with Bion, with his insistence on the importance of being able to change 'vertices' or points of view, and thus see things afresh, as one can in dreams. Indeed, dream, for the later Bion, is the generative core of all our thinking and relating, and dream is the most important keyword of all.

Independently of each other, Winnicott and Bion were the most important contributors to a seismic shift in psychoanalytic theory and practice, amounting to the kind of paradigm change Thomas Kuhn identified in the history of science (Kuhn 1962; Ferro and Civitarese 2015, p. 5). Ferro and his colleagues have registered its force and put it to work – Ferro has equated Bion's impact to that of the French Revolution (Ferro [2014] 2019, p. 56), although Bion's wish was not so much to destroy as to bring out psychoanalysis's untapped potential (Ferro and Civitarese 2015, p. xiv). Thomas Ogden has characterised it as the move from an 'epistemological' psychoanalysis 'having to do with knowing and understanding', represented Freud and Klein – a psychoanalysis of insight and knowledge, involving suspicion, detective work, and decoding – to a psychoanalysis 'having to do with being and becoming'. This 'ontological' psychoanalysis allows the patient 'the experience of creatively discovering meaning for himself, and in that state of being, becoming more fully alive' (Ogden 2019, p. 661). It is a shift of emphasis from content to function, from the *what* to the *how* (Ferro and Civitarese 2015, p. xv), in which the emphasis is less on the interpretation of the dream than on the experience of dreaming; the interpersonal field becomes a 'field of dreams'.

This paradigm requires 'a mental attitude of openness to the new', rather than a 'religious' outlook. It is 'a way of proceeding that can never take its tools for granted and consider then definitive; it is forced to engage in continual self-reflection' (Ferro and Civitarese 2015, pp. xiv and xv). Optimally both patient and analyst exercise and develop their capacities for feeling and thinking, playing and relating – in the face of opposing forces, internal and external. 'It's such a frightful business', said Bion, 'to retain your freshness of mind' (Bion 2005, p. 109).

This epistemological and technical shift has had a particular resonance in Italy, the Italy of Dante and Leopardi, or Fellini, for whom film-making was a form of dreaming, and Eco, who shared with Fellini a joy in the sheer pleasure, the serious play, of storytelling – for as Ferro has said, 'tell me a story' and 'listen to me' are 'two inexhaustible sources of well-being' (Ferro [2010] 2015, p. 56).

There is further fertile ground in the Italian culture of hospitality: an invitation into someone's home opens the prospect of something both to be enjoyed and to be taken very seriously. Ferro conceives of an analytic space hospitable to unexpected guests, indeed to the strangest, the most alien of strangers, who might find a respectful welcome and take pleasure in the food, drink, and conversation on offer. The linguistic template for the conversation is Italian, in which the verb *sentire*, 'to hear' or 'to listen', also means 'to feel' and 'to sense'.

Ferro has been in the mainstream of psychoanalytic life in Italy and internationally for over three decades and is probably more responsible than anyone for putting Italian psychanalysis on the world map (Conci 2019, pp. 295

and 400). He is also a plain-speaking critic of psychoanalysis and its 'high-ranking fundamentalists' (Ferro [2014] 2019, p. 100). 'In my opinion', he has written, 'it is a miracle that psychoanalysis has survived its tendency to put forward certain over-interpretive readings, its inability to grasp the freshness and immediacy of a communication' (Ferro [2010] 2015, p. 56). At the same time, he has always been committed to engaging with other analytic modalities and learning from them.

He will often speak for himself in the following pages, so here is his own summary of his working position.

> Bion says that in each session we should always give the patient a good reason to come back the next time. In other words, the patient should play, have fun, enjoy it … there has to be a Scheherazade function always able to tell new stories, new tales, new metabolizations: a new game. It should be a game, that can be at times sad, at times happy, at times funny, at times tragic. I'm not saying 'game' to diminish its emotional impact: a game can be a really serious thing. The patient should always receive from us a good reason to come the next day … it means activating her curiosity, the pleasure of curiosity.
>
> (Ferro and Nicoli [2017] 2018, pp. 8–9)

Reading Ferro

Ferro is a prolific writer. Pepweb lists 159 articles since 1985, translated into several languages, with many more papers in edited books. His 17 books so far in English translation, written alone or in collaboration, are listed in the references. Where Lacan, Winnicott, and Bion are often gnomic, in a way that signals the importance and originality of what they have to say, Ferro is usually immensely readable. There is no question as to the rigour and penetration of his thinking, but he does not intimidate. His writing typically has the atmosphere of a down-to- earth and often humorous conversation, with a modest, intelligent, and informed interlocutor.

At the heart of his thinking, practice, and writing is metaphor, and this in his words is 'consonant with a psychoanalysis understood as a development of narrations or opening up of possible worlds' (Ferro and Civitarese 2015, p. 11). Among Ferro's favourite metaphors are the kitchen and the restaurant, and cinema and film (Ferro [2002] 2013, p. 99).

> I believe that images, like pictures, are intrinsically polysemic in character. It also seems to me that patients themselves, when they make use of the visual, seem to be perceiving with intensity what we are communicating to them. Sometimes an image can be more effective and communicate more than a long speech.
>
> (Ferro and Pizzuti 2001, para 114)

His writing is also rich in allusions to theatre and literature, including detective stories and science fiction: to Balzac, Hugo, Borges, Pirandello, Calvino, Thomas Harris, Tahar Ben Jelloun, Dante, and Shakespeare, as well as to studies in literary and narrative theory such as those of Propp, Todorov, and Eco, alongside reference to an extraordinary range of psychoanalytic sources.

Sometimes illustrated with the drawings of child patients, his work is full of case vignettes, of varying lengths.

Generally I do not start with the aim of seeking confirmation for theories – perhaps because I want to avoid being shipwrecked on the reefs of saying 'that's what Freud said'. I try instead to use clinical narratives to open up the path to provisional ongoing hypotheses, and … to offer ample margins for discussion and possible dissent.

(Ferro [2007] 2011, p. 172)

Ferro's texts seem to grow organically, like an 'on-going thinking process' (Ogden [2002] 2013, p. ix). 'We might well say about Ferro's exposition that in many respects, the medium is the message' (Renik 2013, pp. ix and x).

For Ferro 'a good book of psychoanalysis … should have the same effect on the reader as chivalrous romances had on "Don Quixote": it should transport us into another dimension' (Ferro [2007] 2011, p. 93). It should have 'the power to kindle a mood of curiosity and passion that makes us say, as we lie in bed at night, "I'll put the light out in a moment" – not once but many times' (ibid., p. 89). It should 'fire the "imagination" and meet the "taste" of the reader: that is, it must inspire delight and pleasure' (ibid., p. 94).

Readers looking for a first-hand introduction might turn to *The New Analyst's Guide to the Galaxy: Questions about Contemporary Psychoanalysis* (Ferro and Nicoli (2017) 2018, original title *Pensieri di uno psicoanalista irreverente*, thoughts of an irreverent psychoanalyst)

Co-written in the form of questions and answers with a younger colleague, it is the most personal and outspoken of Ferro's books. His frequent practice of writing collaboratively invites a collaborative way of reading, a kind of mental/emotional work akin to gymnastics, or Tai-Chi.

His work can bring a feeling of lightness and relief from the superego pressure that can so easily oppress psychoanalytic writers, readers, practitioners, and, as Ferro would point out, patients. His writing is like a sort of algorithm for the experience of an analysis: digressive, elliptical, allusive, sometimes requiring intense mental and emotional labour, sometimes deeply moving. It invites one into a constant process of refinement and expansion of understanding, as the same ground is revisited but each time from a slightly different 'vertex'. He will slip off in new and surprising directions. An essay on anorexia and bulimia turns into a searing meditation on time and mortality (Ferro (ed.) [2016] 2020, pp. 3–13). One can be aware, joining him in the vicissitudes of his thinking and clinical experience, of undergoing cerebral-emotional micro-transformations. The reader 'shares in that experience, is enriched by it, and … transformed him - or herself' (Renik 2002, p. x).

'Ferro's writing skills', wrote Anna Ferruta, 'are like those of a great musician who can allow himself virtuosities while never for a moment forgetting, or lessening, the technical clarity of his performance' (Ferruta 2003, p. 460, cited in Conci 2019, p. 296) Ferro himself is fond of the parallel between writing and painting.

> I have always considered the writing of psychoanalysis (and the experience of being inside an analytic session)

very similar to the activity of a painter, someone intent on making verbal pictures that undergo constant
change, construction and deconstruction both in colours and forms ... In my way of thinking about paint-
ing/writing I have always regarded as fundamental the
'tonight we improvise' approach and the 'taste for not
knowing where you are going'.

(Ferro [2007] 2011, p. 94)

Ferro's relationship to writing is multifaceted. He ha-
bitually revisits his case notes and vignettes, review-
ing sessions 'after a lapse of some years ... to see what
changes in theory and technique I have "made my own"
in the interim' (Ferro [1996] 2002, p. 88). In this he follows the example of Bion, who envisaged his 'Grid' as a
creative game to be taken up after the session. Some of
Ferro's books also end with supervision exercises for the
reader ([2007] 2011; [2010] 2015). His writing is a way
of 'thinking the unthinkable' (Ferro [2007] 2011, Chapter
7), with the inspiration of Bion's *Memoir of the Future* in
the background; *Reveries* ([2008] 2015a) is a collection of
his own waking and sleeping dreams, of varying lengths,
that can surprise and shock.

Is there a difference between what I write, and what I
really think and do in the consulting room? As a rule,
I see what I write as already old and obsolete, but still
needing to be shared with my colleagues. In my office,
I always try to breathe life into something new that I do
not yet know, and that gradually becomes layered and
takes on a shape that can be shared in new concepts.

(Ferro [2010] 2105, p. 524)

He has, however, concluded: 'I would not feel comfortable considering myself a writer, although I've certainly written many things' (Ferro and Civitarese, 2022, p. 387).

Note

1 The field concept 'represents the best way to try to keep track of all the variables of our work, which go well beyond the simple phenomenology of the patient doing the speaking and the analyst doing the interpreting – as Freud himself well knew'.

(Conci 2019, p. 395)

Chapter 1

Foundations

Psychoanalysis in Italy

Ferro's career and international reputation need to be seen in relation to the particular 'parabola' (Conci 2019, p. 462) of the history of Italian psychoanalysis. Psychoanalysis entered Italy by way of Trieste – which was part of the Austro-Hungarian Empire until it joined Italy at the end of the First World War – thanks to two psychiatrists, Marco Levi Bianchini and Edoardo Weiss. Weiss had studied in Vienna, met Freud and been analysed by Paul Federn. Despite Freud's personal love of Italy (he made 20 visits) and his identification of it as the 'locus of the unconscious' (Haddad and Haddad 1995), psychoanalysis was relatively slow to take root in the peninsular. There are several possible reasons for this: the powerful opposition of Catholic culture; the pervasive influence, since the late nineteenth century, of the idealist, anti-positivist philosophy of Benedetto Croce and his followers; and the dominance, in psychiatry, of the organicist thinking of Cesare Lombroso and his theory of 'psychic degeneration' (Civitarese and Ferro 2020, pp. 110–111, and see Caldwell 2016, p. 679 et seq.).

DOI: 10.4324/9781003313311-2

In Italy, furthermore, as Sergio Benvenuto wrote in 1997, 'the highest model for an Italian intellectual was and is, even today, political commitment in the agora' (as, for example, Elena Ferrante's novels attest). This stems perhaps from a long historicist tradition (Vico, De Sanctis, Croce, Gentile, Gramsci), with its basic assumption that it is History with a capital H rather than internal constitution that shapes us. This too may be a factor in Italy's relatively slow uptake of psychoanalysis (Benvenuto 1997, p. 3).

The Società Psicoanalitica Italiana (SPI) was founded in 1925 and reconstituted in 1932; in 1938, psychoanalysis was banned by the Fascist regime. After the Second World War, the Society was re-established by a handful of practitioners. Conditions in Italy never favoured the development of a national 'school'.

The country's geographical shape and the persistence of strong regional identities and linguistic markers undoubtedly also play a part in this. The SPI is composed of local centres, 13 in 2023, each centre having its own clinical and theoretical characteristics (Di Chiara 2016, p. 13; Caparrota and Colazzo Hendriks 2022, p. xii). For Stefano Bolognini in 2001, at that time President of the SPI, the

> multifaceted view is the main characteristic of contemporary Italian psychoanalysis, differentiating it from other national trends (like the French, for instance), characterised by a more uniform perspective. We consider this variety a source of richness and not an effect of pure imitation, because it enriches the internal dialogue among colleagues.
>
> (In Caparrota and Colazzo Hendriks 2022, p. xii)

One psychoanalytic theory with a standard fixed technical model never dominated in Italy. Instead, Italian psychoanalysis always kept in mind the interplay of the individual and society. Leaning more toward the left, Italian analysts were strongly interested in Marx, philosophy and applied psychoanalysis. And, tangential to psychoanalysis, the work of Orlando, Lavaggetto, and Eco played an important role in Italian culture. These authors applied semiology and narrative in analysing important psychoanalytic texts, expanding the concept of interpretation in psychoanalysis. A new formation of Italian analysts began challenging some of the classic views, and some of them began to follow the new American theoretical models.

(Di Donna 2005, p. 43, cited in Conci 2019, pp. 458–459)

Ferruta has noted the multilingual character of Italian psychoanalysis following its relative post-war isolation from the international analytic community. This, she has suggested 'favoured receptivity and the wish to learn from others, with no hesitation and no prejudice' (Ferruta 2016, pp. 23–24, in Conci 2019, p. 458). Local circumstances may thus have had their advantages: Italian analysts born after the war and training during the last quarter of the century did not have to contend with a weight of institutionalised tradition. Obliged to look abroad, they have perhaps been freer than their northern European and Anglo-Saxon counterparts to think, critique, and enquire afresh and for themselves. Multilingualism is 'not only a historical feature, but a specific theoretical element' that has allowed Italian analysts to 'accommodate several approaches to the unconscious with sufficient accuracy and diversification' (Ferruta 2016, pp. 23–24, in Conci 2019, p. 458). In 2001, Ferro noted several coexisting perspectives within Italian psychoanalysis: orthodox Freudians, Kleinians and post-Kleinians, Kohutians, and inter-subjectivists of the American school (Ferro and Pizzuti 2001, para 41).

Translation too was a vital stimulus. Work on the 12-volume Italian edition of Freud's work, edited by Cesare Musatti, started in 1966 and was completed in 1980. Meanwhile Italian analysts were variously editing translations, of Klein (Franco Fornari), Anna Freud and Winnicott (Eugenio Gaddini), Ferenczi (Glauco Carloni), and post-Kleinians such as Racker, Meltzer, Rosenfeld, and especially Bion, by Francesco Corrao (Ferruta 2016, p. 12). Only Brazil, Ferro has noted, has surpassed Italy in terms of the number of translations of foreign authors (Ferro and Pizzuti 2001, para 39).

In the 1960s and 1970s, interest was mainly in French writers, and from the 1970s, starting with Rosenfeld, in the British school (Ferro and Pizzuti 2001, para 40). Kleinian theory in general and the concept of projective identification in particular gradually came to constitute a key area of development (Ferruta 2016, pp. 24–25). From the 1970s, French and then British analysts accepted invitations to conduct seminars in Italy: Bion, Bollas, Milner, Rosenfeld, and Meltzer. The presence of Matte Blanco, who had moved from Chile and settled in Rome in 1966, encouraged further contacts with Latin American analysts. Italian analysts brought to such meetings 'a wealth of clinical material to be perused in an atmosphere of enthusiasm and creative learning'. Their starting point was clinical rather than ideological, and the resulting 'fertile dialectic between practice and theory' has led to developments in Italy that have grown 'increasingly ... autonomous from their sources' and to the creation of genuine theories (Conci 2019, p. 401).

Ferro was later to write:

> it has always been important for me to understand the scientific positions of the Other ... I have had the privilege to work with colleagues from all parts of the world, who followed all kinds of orientations. I always appreciated the points of view they had to offer, which did not prevent me from having positions, sometimes very precise, of my own.
>
> (Ferro 2011)

In 1955, Francesco Corrao had been the first Italian analyst to meet Bion. Corrao spent the rest of his life promoting Bion's work in Italy, as well as that of Meltzer and Racker. He got Bion's books promptly translated (*Learning from Experience*, for example, in 1972) and discussed in the 'then rather small' SPI. With the help of Bion's daughter Parthenope Bion Talamo, who had settled in Italy and was practising in Turin, Corrao and the SPI invited Bion to hold seminars in Rome in 1977. Twenty papers engaging with Bion were published in 1981 in a monographic issue of the *Rivista di Psicoanalisi* edited by Pathenope Bion Talamo and Claudio Neri, including an English edition (Conci 2019, pp. 288–289 and 401). For Corrao, Bion's theory of transformations constituted 'the most revolutionary (or catastrophic) transformation' in psychoanalysis.

The psychoanalysis of the 1990s, he hoped, would not be neurobiological nor 'excessively encroached upon by *objectivity* or *subjectivity*', but '*authentically pluralistic* … concerned with the kinesis of affects', '*relativistic* and *differential*' (Corrao 1989, pp. 67–68).

The result of all these developments, from the last decades of the twentieth century, was a reversal of the 'linguistic tide' and a growing bilateral exchange (Ferruta 2016, p. 23). The 1981 *Rivista di Psicoanalisi* monograph on Bion was, according to Marco Conci, the first time that Italian analysts were able to bring the international analytic community into contact with Italian analytic thinking (Conci 2019, p. 401). Ferro's *The Bi-Personal Field* (1992), published in English in 1999, was to be a further turning point (Conci 2019, p. 400).

Ferro's background and career

Antonino Ferro was born in Palermo in 1947, where he grew up and where he obtained a first-class degree in Medicine and Surgery. Palermo was a significant 'psychoanalytic province', thanks to the presence, from 1934, of the Berlin-trained analyst Alessandra Tomasi di Lampedusa, who had married the author of *Il Gattopardo* (*The Leopard*); the city also helped foster the development of Corrao among other important figures (Civitarese and Ferro 2020, p. 111).

But it was the north that shaped Ferro as an analyst. He specialised in psychiatry in Pavia, just south of Milan. Pavia is a small town with an ancient university and a famous medical school; many of the faculty's psychiatrists were also analysts. Ferro worked with two important teachers in particular: Dario De Martis, who was among Italian psychiatrists/analysts influenced by Rosenfeld and by the insight that the projective flows between patient and analyst are both communicative and a product of the couple at work (Ferruta 2016. p. 25); and Fausto Petrella, who was developing a metaphor of mind as theatre and was, like De Martis, a critic of institutionalised hospital psychiatry (Borgogni, Luchetti and Coe 2016, p. 173). As well as working in Milan, Ferro has continued to live and practise in Pavia, alongside a lively group of analysts including Giuseppe Civitarese, Fulvio Mazzacane, Giovanni Foresti, Maurizio Collovà, Elena Molinari, and Pierluigi Politi (see Mazzacane 2018), and in partnership with other colleagues across Italy and an expanding community of field-sensitive practitioners across the world (the USA, the UK, Israel, Latin, and South America).

Ferro trained and qualified as an analyst during what became known as the 'Italian Renaissance' of psychoanalysis (Di Donna 2005, p. 43; Di Chiara 2016, p. 14). 'At the time when I made my choice', wrote one analyst,

the atmosphere surrounding psychoanalysis was very different from the current climate. At the end of the 1970s, and even more conspicuously in the early 1980s, our discipline was in full bloom, at least in Italy, and featured increasingly in university curricula across the country, both in medicine and in the humanities.

(Borgogno and Capello 2011, p. 95)

Ferro had personal and didactic analyses in the Milan Centre of Psychoanalysis – 'a real breeding ground of psychoanalytic creativity' (Ferruta 2016, p. 27) – with, among others, Giuseppe di Chiara (Conci 2019, p. 401), an analyst especially interested in theorising the analytic relationship (Ferruta 2016, p. 27). Ferro's training was predominantly Kleinian; but he was also supervised by analysts who were touched by the climate of openness and curiosity about developments abroad: Eugenio Gaburri, whose investigations into Bion and the relationship between his clinical work and Freud's metapsychology led to an important collaboration (Ferro and Gaburri 1988; Borgogno, Luchetti and Coe 2016, p. 614), and Luciana Nissim Momigliano (Ferro and Donna 2005, p. 92).

Nissim Momigliano was a paedriatician from a Jewish family who had fought with the partisans in the war and, like her friend Primo Levi, had survived Auschwitz (Conci 2019, p. 480). Her paper 'Two people talking in a room', of 1984, Bionian and relational in focus, was widely influential: analytic work, she wrote, is always a two-way affair, and the patient is the analyst's best colleague. The analyst's mental functioning, her capacity for reverie, and her respect for the patient are essential (Nissim Momigliano and Robutti 1992, pp. 5–20; Ferruta 2016, p. 27). Nissim published two early co-written papers by Ferro in a co-edited volume of her own (Bezoari and Ferro, and Barale and Ferro, in Nissim Momigliano and Robutti 1992; Ferruta 2016, p. 28).[1]

Ferro would also have been schooled in a particular form of attention: generations of Italian analysts have been trained to monitor every moment of the session, including 'modification of sensations, atmospheres and bodily experiences', accurately following every tiny exchange (Neri 2009, p. 47). An analyst, Ferro has said, should also have had 'experience of various models (in particular Freud, Klein, Bion) so as to be able to stand at a distance from them and develop a personal creativity and personal points of view' (2015c, p. 187). For each model has 'its own truth (or rather, its own approach to the truth)' (Ferro [1992] 1999, p. 18), an attitude that will certainly have informed his own teaching, at Pavia University's Psychiatric Centre and at Milan University, where for many years he was professor of Child Psychoanalysis and Psychotherapy.

Since the start of his practice, Ferro was interested in the analysis of children and adolescents as well as of seriously troubled patients, and this too needs to be seen in an Italian context. Under the stimulus of exposure to Klein's pioneering work (Klein [1932] 1997 and [1961] 1998), child analysis, together with family analysis, assumed a special importance in Italy in the 1970s and 1980s, and took original directions, particularly in Milan (Ferruta 2016, pp. 31–33). Analytic work with children was also stimulated by Eugenio and Renata Gaddini in Rome, who were friends and collaborators with Winnicott.

In psychiatry, from the late 1970s onwards, the work of Franco Basaglia and *Psichiatria Democratica* had a tremendous impact, leading, through the 1978 Legge Basaglia, to the closure of the old, often brutal psychiatric hospitals, or *manicomi* (Foot 2015). Basaglia was certainly among the politically committed, a psychiatrist and revolutionary for whom psychoanalysis was a bourgeois science. But the shift of the centre of gravity of mental heath provision away from the hospital and towards community mental health centres also worked, for analysts and therapists, as a 'call to care' (Ferruta 2016, p. 35) for a whole population of formerly invisible patients. It was 'an important and influential experience for many [psychoanalytic] colleagues over several generations' that 'enriched the psychotherapeutic dimension of our psychiatry' (Conci 2019, pp. 457 and 554).

In Pavia, Ferro's teachers and colleagues Dario De Martis and Fausto Petrella were among those directly involved in the reform project, as was Eugenio Gaburri in Varese. The presence in Pavia of psychiatrists who were, relatively uncommonly, also psychoanalysts attracted a generation of young psychiatrists who wished to work analytically, and this led, over two succeeding generations, to the development of a Pavia 'school' (Mazzacane, personal communication, 2023).

Generally speaking, Italian psychoanalysis's understanding of psychotic states 'may be one of its most articulated contributions, because it infused theoretical ideas into the complex areas of community mental health, institutions, and group processes' (Di Donna 2005, p. 48). Between 1976 and 1983, Ferro worked with the National Research Centre on a project aimed at the Prevention of Mental Diseases; perhaps this early focus on the 'seeds of health' was close to that held by Bion and Rickwood in their work at Northfield in the Second World War, about which Ferro might by then have known. It is likely to have furthered the development of a collaborative, bi- or multi-personal approach, and of the idea of a co-created field.

'My model and technique', Ferro later summarised,

> arose from work with severe pathologies (borderline
> and psychotic patients, as well as children) ... [and] my
> technical approach can be extrapolated also to neurotic
> patients, at least if we wish to reach and explore the
> deepest level of their minds, where we discover *lumps*
> of severe pathology (which may be psychotic, border-
> line, or autistic). With all patients, I consider that the
> purpose of analysis is to work not so much on insight,
> the overcoming of splits, repression, or historical re-
> construction, as on the development of the instruments
> for thinking.
>
> (Ferro 2015a, p. 152)

'I studied the thought of Bion with great passion' (Ferro
2011).

Ferro's Kleinian development

Ferro has described himself as a 'repentant Kleinian' – in
two respects.

> I consider (a) that the negotiation of Kleinian thought
> and technique is essential in training; and (b) that one
> needs to *recover* from this approach, especially as re-
> gards the constant decoding of unconscious fantasies
> and the risk of 'simultaneous translation' of what a pa-
> tient says.
>
> (Ferro 2015a, p. 512)

Here is how he accounts for his move away from his
Kleinian roots.

I keep changing following some tips that I get directly or indirectly from my patients … a patient came to me and said, 'Now I have to have a serious talk with you. I have no intention of lying down on the couch, I have to tell you something really important instead. When I arrived in your office, I had a problem. That problem was my boyfriend. After I left at the end of the session, I found myself with two problems: one with my boyfriend, and the second one with you. I wonder, what was my mistake?'

This episode goes back to when I was a Kleinian, and I interpreted everything transferentially. This event was very important to me, because it allowed me to distance myself from the obligation to continually interpret transference. It became important to me to highlight the transformations that occurred in the session, instead of translating immediately what the patient said about her boyfriend in a transference interpretation. This opened my mind to the idea that the most important thing was to transform the relationship of the patient with her boyfriend. But in my mind, the boyfriend was me, without a doubt.

Except, I no longer felt the need to remind the patient that the boyfriend was me … In my mind – in the kitchen – it was me.

(Ferro and Nicoli [2017] 2018, pp. 88–89)

He has characterised this situation, especially within British Kleinianism, as 'a disease called "compulsive transference interpretation"' (Ferro [2006] 2009, p. 171). The realization that it was necessary to speak to patients in such a way that they really felt helped was the basis for what he and a colleague, Michele Bezoari, began to call 'narrative' or 'weak' interpretations (Bezoari and Ferro, 1989; Ferro 2013, p. 110).

On what else, alongside learning from experience, did this shift rest? The answer is, in large part, Bion. So what is the theoretical basis, Bionian and otherwise, for this emphasis on 'highlighting the transformations that occur in the session'? And, it would seem from this example, doing something that at first sight, from a British Kleinian point of view, might seem highly 'unpsychoanalytic'? For Ferro seems intent on attending to the real-life relationship with the boyfriend, to the point even of 'transforming' it (this would be what he later calls a 'transformation in narrative' (Ferro 2018b).

His approach certainly respects the factuality of the patient's account and what is most urgently on her mind, with no immediate reference to the supposed state of her internal world. As Ferro will go on to assert later, it is 'an inalienable right of the patient to think that when she speaks of her husband she is "really" talking about her husband, and not of a split aspect of herself' (Ferro [2010] 2015, p. 130).

In fact, the foundations of Ferro's approach *are* firmly grounded in Klein and the Kleinian notions of 'unconscious phantasy' (Isaacs 1948) and 'psychic reality' (Ferro [1992] 1999, pp. 6–10). But it evolved out of the ways in which Bion – who after all began his psychoanalytic career as a Kleinian and had been analysed by Klein – developed these ideas in clinical practice. And it found its mature form with the introduction of the concept of the analytic field, as first formulated by the French-Argentinian analysts Willy and Madeleine Baranger. This was, moreover, already latent in Bion's thinking.

The birth of Post-Bionian Field Theory, or BFT: Bion, the Barangers, and the field

As far as Civitarese can discern (Civitarese 2023, p. 3), the 'birth of BFT' was marked in a paper of 1989, 'Listening, Interpretations and Transformative Functions in the Analytical Dialogue', co-written by Ferro and Michele Bezoari and published simultaneously in Italian and in English (Bezoari and Ferro 1989). Bringing Bion and the Barangers together for the first time, the paper offers a privileged glimpse of an analytic philosophy *in statu nascendi.*

The authors report that (as we have already seen) some patients 'seemed not to tolerate interpretations of transference explicitly expressed as such, not even with all the gradualness, delicacy and timeliness we were capable of' (Bezoari and Ferro 1989, p. 1022). They seemed to feel that the more explicit the analyst's need to communicate, the more threatening it was, and responded accordingly. Enrico dreams of a desert island where an unseen person is firing shots at his head. Maria, after an interpretation clearly intended to bring relief, announces that she must be careful; there are the Fascists with clubs, ready to beat people up. Giulio dreams of a sentry on guard duty who starts shooting wildly after being approached peaceably.

Such patients, Bezoari and Ferro found, 'could better tolerate the same interpretations as long as they were "*clothed*"', that is, 'expressed the same contents as a transference interpretation … but which we "dressed up" in words and representations borrowed from the discourse of the patient', without explicit 'here and now' references.

When they were not faced with a sudden change in the expressive level upon which they had placed the communication, the patients seemed more willing to venture gradually, in the moment and manner which they themselves indicated (for example through dreams), into the territory of transference implications.

(Bezoari and Ferro 1989, p. 1024)

'It was not my job to give this link to my patient in this session', wrote Winnicott in *Playing and Reality*, 'because the patient is essentially at a stage of discovering things for herself, and premature interpretation in such circumstances annihilates the creativity of the patient and is traumatic in the sense of being against the maturational process.' (Winnicott 1971, p. 137) Bezoari and Ferro do not directly reference Winnicott in their paper, but his presence can be felt, and echoes of him will be heard throughout Ferro's work.

Contact with the 'naked truth', Bezoari and Ferro continue, can inflict pain upon patients, 'or on any one of us'; interpretative formulations, 'the means by which that truth is approached', must be adapted 'to the level of tolerance and sensitivity of each individual patient' (Bezoari and Ferro 1989, p. 1024). The authors are reminded of a passage in Marguerite Duras's *La douleur*, about a concentration camp survivor who 'couldn't eat without dying. But he couldn't go on not eating without dying' (Duras 1985, pp. 56–60. Bezoari and Ferro 1989, pp. 1024–1026). The analyst, like a mother with her child, must be able to guess and evaluate how much stimulation and suffering the patient can bear.

Figure 2 'And that's nothing! I know some even more in-
teresting interpretations!' – 'Poor me!' A scene
from a comic book brought to a session by ten-
year-old Marina (In Ferro ([1992] 1999), *The Bi-
Personal Field. Experiences in Child Analysis*. London
and New York: Routledge, p. 34, fig. 2.10).

> We realized ... that the adjustments made to our techni-
> cal instruments, in the search for a better approach to
> our 'difficult' patients, was gradually modifying both
> our clinical practice and our more general ideas about
> interpretation. At a certain stage of our journey ... we
> felt the need to re-read and re-order the theoretical map
> of the psychoanalytical field in which we were moving.
> (Bezoari and Ferro 1989, p. 1028)

Not only were interventions that were intended to prepare
the patient for a true transference interpretation 'received
with relief and receptiveness'. They also elicited responses
which actively contributed to a continuing transformative
process, often in unforeseen directions. 'For the very fact
of not having gone too far ... in making ... enunciations
which were too assertive, we felt freer to explore these
new directions with the patients, gradually modifying our

initial ideas'. In this way, the analytic dialogue became less 'a field for the gathering of data and the verification of … hypotheses' than

> a kind of forge, where interpretations acquire *form and sense* thanks to a *hermeneutic cooperation* in which the patient possesses equal, though not symmetrical, dignity of functions, and is the analyst's *best colleague* in the full meaning of the term (Bion 1983).
>
> (Bezoari and Ferro 1989, pp. 1028–1030)

Analytic listening, the authors write, involves what the patient says passing through the 'prism' of the analyst's mind, whose facets include his own personal and unconscious qualities and characteristics and the cultural components of his professional identity, including the theoretical options available to him. A process of refraction, of semantic disassembling, takes place, which produces certain directions or lines of thought. Now the analyst may univocally choose to follow one line, or 'he may involve the patient in the choice, by supplying a communication which is only partially codified and which therefore presents various possible directions to be taken' (Bezoari and Ferro 1989, p. 1030). Such would be a '*weak*' or '*unsaturated*' interpretation, 'with respect to which the patient's contribution is not simply an accessory, but is indispensable for forming the sense'. The analyst is now no longer the 'sole depository of power and hermeneutic competence'. The emphasis has shifted to the 'profoundly *intersubjective* and *dialogical* nature of the interpretative work which is achieved in this way' (Bezoari and Ferro 1989, p. 1032).

This 'laxer construction of the analytic dialogue' and 'freer fluctuation of sense' were, moreover,

> reminiscent of atmospheres and dynamics typical to group situations. Referring back to Bion's notion of the groupality within the individual, leads us to consider the mental state from which these 'weak interpretations' originate as a functioning presence, in the analyst, of an *internal work group*, capable of making its listening sensitive to a wider range of tones, and of attributing responses with a *polyphonic* resonance ... the analyst-patient couple itself can be thought of as a *two-person work group* (Meltzer 1986).
>
> (Bezoari and Ferro 1989, p. 1032)

Ferro and Bezoari had noted how Bion focussed on the analyst's mental functioning in the session – the containing function of reverie, in particular – and how (in the footsteps of Joseph, Segal, and other Kleinian colleagues) Bion extended the concept of countertransference to include 'the globality of the analyst's emotions, the unavoidable, essential terrain in which interpretative thought takes root' (Bezoari and Ferro 1989, p. 1020). At the same time, the authors continue, Bion stressed that projective identification was not just a symptom of pathology but also had a communicative function. The next sequence in the article follows seamlessly.

'Thus, the analytical situation comes to be conceived of as a *bipersonal field* (Baranger and Baranger 1966), and emphasis is placed upon the spiral-like progression of the analytical dialogue'. The authors acknowledge that this idea was also implicit in the thinking of Ferro's supervisor

Nissim Momigliano (1984), and in the work of Robert Langs in the U.S. a decade earlier (Langs was, from 1976, the first to champion the Barangers' work outside South America; Langs 1977). For the Barangers, Bezoari and Ferro write, if the analytic situation is regarded as a bipersonal field, everything in it must have a bipersonal dimension, including interpretation and insight. We shall leave their paper with this quotation from the Barangers:

> The insight that is specifically analytic is that process of joint comprehension by analyst and patient of an unconscious aspect of the field ... that is, of an element of the 'bipersonal unconscious fantasy' active in that moment.
>
> (Baranger and Baranger 1966, p. 385, in Bezoari and Ferro 1989, p. 1033)

The field, in the Barangers' formulation,

> cannot ... be considered to be the *sum* of the two internal situations. It is something created *between* the two, within the unit that they form in the moment of the session, something radically different from what each of them is separately.'
>
> (Baranger and Baranger, 1961–1962, in Eizirik 2009, p. xi)[2]

Although other analysts, notably H.S. Sullivan in the U.S., had adumbrated field ideas in their work (Conci 2019), the Barangers, who took some of their inspiration from Heinrich Racker and Enrique Pichon-Rivière, were the first to use the field concept as the foundation for a thoroughly new model in psychoanalysis (Civitarese 2023, p. 1). Their classic paper was published in the same years, 1961–62, that Winnicott and Bion were laying the foundations of a radically intersubjective psychoanalytic theory of the birth of the psyche. The paper did not cite Bion, but Madeleine Baranger later acknowledged his longstanding influence on their thinking. His studies on small groups, she wrote, showed the field to be more than a matter of intersubjective relations; the Barangers' 'basic unconscious fantasy', deriving partly from Bion's 'basic assumption', was something created by the field situation itself (Baranger 2004, and see Civitarese and Ferro 2009, p. 192, and Sabbadini and Ferro 2010). Thus what happens in the bipersonal field will not simply be a repetition, because it arises in a new context (Cassorla 2005, p. 802).

In Italy the concept of the field continued its own evolution and received decisive impetus from Francesco Corrao. Corrao, who was also a pioneer of group psychotherapy, gave great weight to Bion's focus on the functioning of the analyst's mind as a transformative factor within the analytic relationship (Ferruta 2016, p. 25). Emphasising the group dimension, Corrao saw the field as the 'sum of the patient's and the analyst's internal group dynamics', giving rise to an extended group situation. There is no analysis between two people, Corrao said; each analysis involves a group consisting of the characters that emerge in the session, who are jointly created by patient and analyst (Ferro and Nicoli [2017] 2018, p. 87, and see Corrao 1986a, 1986b, 1987). Corrao's original thinking was profoundly important for Ferro (see too Ferro [2002] 2013, p. 34).

Ferro will find himself devoting the rest of his career to exploring and elaborating the field idea. He had been developing the concept pragmatically from early on, 'meanwhile discovering that the notion was already outlined by the Barangers, Bion and Corrao' (Ferro [1992] 1999, pp. 180–181). It is the organising 'thought waiting for thinker', the means by which he is able to give a new and original working description, itself in a process of constant evolution, to the phenomenological polyphony of the analytic encounter.

Some further psychoanalytic groundwork

The theory of the field, as Bion's analyst and colleague John Rickman wrote, is 'capable of incommoding one's complacency' (Rickman cited in Conci 2019, p. 337).[3] How could it not? Individualistic ways of thinking about ourselves and our relations to each other have been entrenched in Western consciousness since at least the seventeenth century. In this model, at its crudest, we are sovereign, individual subjectivities, communicating with each other across some inert aether. Even Freud, for all the attention he paid to the group, to culture and civilization, and for all his insistence that we are subject to an 'unknown' and can thus no longer claim to be 'masters in our own houses' (Freud 1917, p. 143), finally returns us to an individualistic view, to an idea of 'the unconscious' as a personal possession, which is hard to shift. There may be unconscious-to-unconscious communication, but attention tends to focus on the effect one has on the other, rather than on the possibility of a form of unconscious which is co-generated, and in which

> subject and object... [r]ather than existing as positive entities, pure presences-in-themselves, except in an abstract sense, ... mould each other in an incessant, fluid to-and-fro traffic of sensations.
>
> (Civitarese and Ferro 2013, p. 191)

At least Klein's spatial conception of the internal world was of a dynamic 'theatre' of mind (Ferro [1992] 1999, p. 7] rather than a purely private enclave. Ferro retains from Klein all that points towards the relational and interpsychic, above all projective identification in the way Bion developed the concept. Projective identification was key to the connection Ferro and Bezoari were increasingly making between the Barangers and Bion, emphasising in an important paper of 1991 how much the Barangers had developed it

> in a direction ... extraordinarily reminiscent of the works of Bion. If projective identification is not only the omnipotent fantasy of an individual, but 'a two-way affair' (Bion 1980), 'it is no surprise that it is of decisive importance in the structuring of every couple' (M. and W. Baranger 1961–62).
>
> (Bezoari and Ferro 1991, p. 16)[4]

Within a field model, the concept of projective identification assumes a powerful explanatory force. It makes visible (Greek *theorein*: 'to see' or 'to contemplate') the communication channels necessary for the establishment of a common, unconscious psychological area, and the 'indispensable points of contiguity' that enable us to influence each other mentally (Ferro and Civitarese 2015, p. 5). Ogden's (1979) emphasis on the strongly relational dimension of projective identification was also significant (Ferro and Civitarese 2015, p. 6).

Ferro found he had little use for those aspects of Kleinian theory that focus on the intrapsychic, the psychological structuring of the individual, particularly the notions of splitting and part objects – and little interest therefore in interpreting from this perspective. Only the paranoid-schizoid and depressive positions had enduring conceptual value for him, but in their Bionian incarnations as alternating poles of emotional possibility, two 'regimes' not just of the individual's but also of the couple's mental functioning. The convergence between Bion's and the Barangers' approaches, Bezoari and Ferro wrote in 1991,

> seems to explain this oscillation without there being any need to ascribe it to the patient's resistances, attacks of envy or negative therapeutic reactions, nor to the analyst's technical errors or personal defects, with the various degrees of apportioning of guilt to one or the other that this implies.
>
> (Bezoari and Ferro 1991, pp. 30–32)

Betty Joseph's model of transference as a 'total situation' (Joseph 1985) was important, particularly regarding its encouragement of reflection on countertransference as a way of seeing how the patient has mobilised the analyst's anxieties. But it was a model still grounded in relationship. The field model, for Ferro, conceives not just of the relationship but the analytic situation as a whole, including the setting and the rules, as a totality:

> This offers us the possibility of thinking that many analytic events 'belong in the consulting room' before they can be referred to the relationship. The analytic space thus becomes a kind of intermediate area where scenes and characters that would otherwise remain immobilised and imprisoned can come to life and find embodiment. Within this framework, the analytic relationship is one of the functions of the field itself.
>
> (Ferro 2005, p. 94)

The field idea involves the analyst in a way that can no longer adequately be conceptualised solely in terms of relationship, let alone of 'transference-countertransference', a sort of ping-pong of projection and identification between two individuals. The model no longer requires the state of the here-and-now relationship to be made explicit in the session; instead, 'the relational aspect in effect becomes a stream flowing through the field; this river then widens out into a vast lake' (Ferro and Basile 2008, p. 2).

The field model as generated by the coming together of the Barangers and Bion was a new departure. The Barangers' theoretical outlook, informed as it also was by Susan Isaacs's concept of unconscious fantasy (1948) and León Grinberg's 'projective counter-identification' (1957) (Ferro and Civitarese 2015, p. 2), still committed them to making 'strong' interpretations of the unconscious phantasy of the couple as it emerged. In addition, there was the assumption that it is always possible to know the moment when anxiety emerges and when to communicate it. Bion, Ferro reminds us, abandoned such certainties, favouring 'weak', 'unsaturated', and open-ended interpretations 'and the continual creation – as opposed to the decoding – of new meanings'. In Bion there is an awareness of the processes and transformations needed when anxiety emerges and a sensitivity to the time it may take, maybe days or months, before an interpretation can be given (Ferro [1992] 1999, pp. 16–17).

Psychoanalysis has done much else to question and undermine the individualistic, two-person model, from Jung's 'collective unconscious' (Jung [1959] 2014) to Winnicott's 'there is no such as an infant' (Winnicott 1960, p. 39, n. 1), Ogden's 'intersubjective analytic third' (Ogden, 1994), Grotstein's 'dreaming ensemble' (Grotstein ([2007] 2018 p. 274), and Green's 'analytic object … formed by the analytic encounter' (e.g. Green 2002, p. 61). Ferro acknowledged his debt to all these conceptualisations. Perhaps encouraged by his supervision with Dina Vallino Macciò, he also set great store on the contribution of José Bleger ([1967] 1990) regarding the 'institutional' nature of the setting and its relation to the formation of the individual's so-called 'meta-ego' (Ferro and Civitarese 2015, p. 6). Here was a further foundation for the field concept, a recognition, paralleling Bion's and Rickwood's, that something larger than interpersonal relationship was needed to allow the emergence of psychotic phenomena, of '*lumps* of severe pathology' (Ferro 2015a, p. 512): the interpersonal field as something that might, like the institution, offer a safe space, asylum, for madness.

Group analysis has developed the concept of a 'social unconscious' (Hopper and Weinberg 2011), and the revolutionary implications of Bion's *Experiences in Groups* are still perhaps fully to be worked out. The particular relation of Bion's book to the field idea is a whole subject in itself (Civitarese 2021). Bezoari and Ferro, we have seen, touched on it in 1989:

> Bion's notion of the groupality within the individual, leads us to consider … a functioning presence, in the analyst, of an *internal work group*, capable of making its listening sensitive to a wider range of tones, and of attributing response with a *polyphonic* resonance.
>
> (Bezoari and Ferro 1989, p. 1032)

The unconscious fantasy of the couple is 'similar to what happens in the case of fantasies emerging in groups' (Bezoari and Ferro 1991, p. 14). The idea of group, of multiplicity, permeates the field concept at every level, including that of the embodiment which we hold in common. What can unequivocally be taken as a field theory appeared in *Experiences in Groups* (Civitarese 2023, p. 1),[5] in which Bion speculated on the existence of a 'proto-metal system', which 'transcends experience', but is the matrix that holds the group together.

> It is from this matrix that emotions proper to the basic assumption flow to reinforce, pervade, and, on occasion, to dominate the mental life of the group. Since it is a level in which physical and mental are undifferentiated, it stands to reason that, when distress from this source manifests itself, it can manifest itself just as well in physical forms as in psychological.
>
> (Bion [1961] 1989, pp. 101–102, cited in Ferro and Civitarese 2015, p. 4)

Thus, as Ogden wrote (2008), when a patient goes into analysis, he so to speak *loses his own mind*. Through re-connecting with 'the re-established proto-mental area', he initiates a deeply involving communication that can work 'to repair dysfunctional places in his internal group con-figuration' (Ferro and Civitarese 2015, p. 6).

Science and philosophy

In his thinking about the field, Corrao underlined Heisen-berg's insight, from the world of quantum physics, that a sharp distinction cannot be drawn between the observer and the objects of investigation; there is always a signifi-cant reciprocal interaction between the observer and the observed (Corrao 1986a), just as for Bion, the observa-tional experience of the analyst was part of the field of observation (Ferro [1992] 1999, p. 11).

Corrao also drew on post-Heideggerian hermeneutics: interpretation arose from a complex field of couple inter-actions in which the participants are bound in a relation-ship of 'hermeneutic reciprocity and complementarity' (Corrao 1986b, 115–116; Bezoari and Ferro 1992a, p. 53; Ferro 2005, p. 90). In this account, each analytic session is, crucially, an ongoing re-narration of the emotional facts of the field (Ferro [1999] 2006, p. 39).

In philosophy the task of loosening our conception of ourselves as bounded individuals has been energeti-cally undertaken by phenomenology and existentialism, above all in the works of Martin Heidegger and of Mau-rice Merleau-Ponty (Ferro and Civitarese 2015, pp. 2–5, and 151–169); Merleau-Ponty was a seminal influence on the Barangers. The ideas of Kurt Lewin in Gestalt psychology (Lewin 1951) and of other social scientists and philosophers of the first half of the twentieth century have been charted by Bazzi (2022), who provides the most comprehensive historical account of overlapping conceptualisations of the field (see too Ferro ([1996] 2013, p. 1); Hinshelwood 2018 and 2023, pp. 30–38, Snell (2021, p. 20 et seq), Civitarese, 2022, etc.). Lewin's importance was acknowledged by Bezoari and Ferro from the start (1991, p. 12); the Barangers also took inspiration from him, but in the second, revised version of their 1961–62 paper (Baranger and Baranger 2008), they replaced Lewin's name with Merleau-Ponty's.

Merleau-Ponty was familiar with Klein's work, and like Klein, he considered that identity can be thought of 'only in terms of difference, of the intersection between the subject's body and the world of things and other people. A person can be himself only by projecting himself outside his own self into the other, and vice versa' (Ferro and Civitarese 2015, p. 27, n. 3). But Klein, with her primary interest in the unconscious and psychic reality, 'disregarded the *carnal*—feeling and felt—aspect of the body (even though the body is absolutely the protagonist of the subject's unconscious fantasies)' (Ferro and Civitarese 2015, p. 160).

The field metaphor is the cornerstone of Merleau-Ponty's philosophy. He conceptualised the absolute interdependence of subject and context, and the constant, reciprocal influence of self and other; following this, one can no longer think of the subject without thinking of the intermediate space between subject and subject (Ferro and Civitarese 2015, p. 160). For Merleau-Ponty, furthermore, consciousness, space, and time are in a dynamic continuity, and they are intimately bound up with our shared corporeality. The subject, he wrote, emerges from 'a substrate of anonymous, pre-reflective and pre-personal intersensoriality / intercorporeality', an 'obscure pre-categorial background [that] ... paves the way for the entry of the transcendental ego on to the world stage'. Regulated by what Merleau-Ponty called the 'porosity of the flesh', subject and object '*co-originate* in a primordial medium to which both belong' (Ferro and Civitarese 2015, pp. 2–3, citing Merleau-Ponty [1945] 2002, p. 473).

Touching something, Merleau-Ponty observed, is at the same time being touched. Our sense of the world is not only an intellectual content, for we cannot dispense with our experience of our bodies; it stems from our fleshly existence and is present even before a consciousness of self forms. Hence, Merleau-Ponty's assertion: '"I am a field, an experience" ([1945] 2002, p. 473)—that is, *a system of relationships*' (Ferro and Civitarese 2015, pp. 2–3). This insistence on the experience of the body led Merleau-Ponty to develop theories 'very close to current notions of the unrepressed, or *sensory*, unconscious' (ibid. p. 27, n. 3). His thinking chimes with Winnicott's, and particularly closely with Bion's. Merleau-Ponty's 'substrate of anonymous, pre-reflective and pre-personal intersensoriality' has parallels with Bion's 'proto-mental area' (Merleau-Ponty [1945] 2002, p. 473; Bion [1961] 1989, pp. 101–102).

Further possibilities were opened up, again with the encouragement of Corrao, and as we shall see later, by linguistics, semiotics, and narrative theory. Nor should we underestimate the impact on Ferro of literature and painting, film and theatre, particularly in their modernist and postmodern forms. Foregrounding the sensory experiences of reading and looking, presenting unreliable narrators, slippages and elisions of meanings, and ever-expanding semantic worlds, such works find new ways to implicate readers and spectators as critics and co-creators.

Play

By the time of the publication of *The Bi-Personal Field* ([1992] 1999), the field idea was becoming integral to Ferro's thinking. *The Bi-Personal Field* is full of startling, moving children's drawings, 'animated like a sort of affective theatre … which generates sense and meaning' (Ferro is quoting from Meltzer 1984). The drawing is less something to be translated or decoded than

> an authentic dream-like photograph of the mental functioning of the couple at a given moment, although taken from a particular and often as yet unknown perspective which we must share in if we are to reach the patient on his own ground.
>
> (Ferro [1992] 1999, p. 23)

Thus, at his first meeting with eight-year-old Marco, Ferro refrains from making a symbolic interpretation of Marco's devouring, oral shark (thus side-stepping the risk of becoming an even more frightening dragon), and comments instead that he and Marco do not yet know much about each other and that, like in the drawing, there is lots beneath the surface of the water for them to discover.

Marco then adds a diver and a ship. Ferro comments that an adventure is unfolding, and maybe there is treasure. Marco picks up 'the affective implication' of this, and suddenly becomes excited, colouring in the up-to-now black and white animals and adding a red and green traffic light, with which he will indicate whether Ferro's suggestions are right or wrong. And it now seems, in the drawing, that something is trying to free itself from the shark's jaws.

Thus, 'an affective-emotional story is set in motion by unleashing emotions and feelings in the couple through the projective identifications that create the treasure which comes to life in the session'. A 'significant, unrepeatable emotional experience is created that draws vitality from the mental work (reverie) which occurs within the couple' – but only if the analyst puts aside schemes and codes 'which might … indicate the availability of "instruments", but not of mental and emotional spaces' (Ferro [1992] 1999, pp. 29–30). For we 'are dealing with a sort of middle ground which may give rise to scenes and characters that would otherwise remain trapped in a premature elucidation of relational movements' (Ferro [1992] 1999, p. 17).

It is significant that *The Bi-Personal Field*, which was so important in bringing Ferro and Italian psychoanalysis to international attention, is about experiences in child analysis. It underlines the element of play: not just as an equivalent to free association in adult speech, a vehicle, as Klein understood it, for carrying unconscious meaning waiting to be decoded, but as a prerequisite for transformation, a de-concretising of 'reality', and a curative experience in itself. Ferro sees no hard and fast distinction between therapy with children and therapy with adults: 'a *psychoanalytic game* I often instigate is to transform a child analysis session with drawings and play into a session with an adult, involving dreams and stories of various kinds, and also vice versa' (Ferro 2015a, p. 519). For the transformational principle – beta to alpha – is the same.

And this – to offer a schematic summary – brings us to the third iteration of the field concept. In the first, that of the Barangers, the analytic situation is a dynamic field in which analyst and patient co-create and share unconscious phantasy in the here and now, and resistance belongs to the couple, not just the patient.

In the second, influenced by narratology and by Corrao, every analysis involves a group of characters that emerge in the session, jointly created by patient and analyst (Corrao 1986a and 1986b; Roos 2020, p. 849).

The third iteration involves the further conjunction of field theory with Bion's 'alpha function' and 'waking dream thought' (Roos 2020, p. 849), to which we now turn.

Notes

1 Another of Ferro's early supervisors, Stefania Turillazzi Manfredi, who was interested in Latin American psychoanalysis as well as the dynamics of listening, may have been the first to introduce the concept of the 'analytic field' into Italy (Borgogno, Luchetti and Coe 2016, p. 209; Ferruta 2016, p. 26).

2 The Barangers' 1962 paper 'The analytic situation as a dynamic field' was only translated from Spanish and published in English in 2008 (Baranger and Baranger 2008).

It was, however, included in the book of 1990 *La situazione psicoanalitica come campo bipersonale* (Baranger and Baranger 1990) edited by Ferro and Stefania Manfredi (Conci 2019, p. 316).

3 'Field' also has disturbing echoes with slavery and the cotton fields, and with white anthropologists doing 'field work'. But perhaps in its post-Bionian context the word can be felt to derive its usefulness as a metaphor from sources other than racism and colonialism.

4 The paper, 'A Journey through the Bipersonal Field', was republished in an expanded form in Nissim Momigliano and Robutti (1992, pp. 43–65).

5 The chapter – described by Lacan as a 'miracle' – was developed from Bion and Rickman's seminal paper of 1943 'Intra-group tensions in Therapy: Their Study as the task of the Group' (Bion and Rickman 1943; Civitarese 2023, p. 1).

Chapter 2

The Bionian dream model

Beta to alpha

'It is not easy to accept that the focus of analysis is on developing the ability to dream and not on working on repression or splits' (Ferro [2010] 2015, p. 142). So in what way is the session, instead, a dream of two minds? Ferro's thinking on this matter stays close to Bion's, so I feel justified in interspersing their words in what follows.

The primitive 'proto-mental' mind that Bion postulated was made up of hypothetical entities that he christened 'beta-elements'. These elements are the sources of our aliveness and our greatest terrors, of storms of feeling which threaten to overwhelm and from which, if we are unable to negotiate them, we must find ways of protecting ourselves. Our aliveness can terrify us. Bion presented these ideas in 1962 in *Learning from Experience*: beta-elements are 'sense impressions and emotions ... not felt to be as phenomena but things in themselves ... undigested facts' (Bion [1962] 1991, pp. 6–7). They are 'primitive pre-thoughts or non-recognized proto-affects that await a mind to think them' (Grotstein 2000, p. 690).

DOI: 10.4324/9781003313311-3

Bion came up with the deliberately 'unsaturated' meta-phor of beta-elements in order to encourage us to imag-ine for ourselves something of the mobile, burgeoning quality of the neonate's inchoate, preverbal, somatic ex-perience. Even after we have started to develop minds, self-awareness, and cognition, we continue to be subject to the life of the body, which most of the time persists beyond our consciousness: psyche does not supplant soma. The two are all the time in complex interaction, as Bion sug-gests in *Experiences in Groups* ([1961] 1989, pp. 101–102) and in *A Memoir of the Future* ([1975, etc.] 1991).

For Ferro, these proto-mental states exert a pressure that can create not just storms but 'tsunamis', explosions of feeling. These eruptions of primitive sensoriality, Ferro insists, crucially distancing himself from Freud and Klein, should never be confused with aggression; aggression is 'a normal faculty of the species … What is in excess is the pressure coming from proto-mental states that plead to be collected, contained and transformed' (Ferro [2007] 2011, p. 6).

For beta-elements are capable of evolution and trans-formation, through what Bion termed 'alpha-function': they can be 'alpha-betized' 'into alpha-elements that can then enter into "mental digestion" as memories, feelings, and thoughts' (Grotstein 2000, p. 690).

… alpha-function whether in sleeping or waking trans-forms the sense-impressions related to an emotional experience, into alpha-elements, which cohere as they proliferate to form the contact barrier. This contact bar-rier marks the point of contact and separation between conscious and unconscious elements and originates the distinction between them.

(Bion [1962] 1991, p. 17)

The 'contact barrier' is in constant formation.

The process of alphabetisation involves the generation of visual images. Ferro has likened alpha-function to a tomato strainer, in which beta-element tomatoes are transformed into pictograms (Ferro [2006] 2009, p. 138). They are proto-thoughts, related to what Bion called 'preconceptions', thoughts on the possible brink of finding a thinker.

These images or pictograms have a dual function, creative and transformational, and protective. Their prototype is the dream image. The dream, Bion wrote,

> makes a barrier against mental phenomena which might overwhelm the patient's awareness … The ability to dream preserves the personality from what is virtually a psychotic state. It therefore helps to explain the tenacity with which the dream, as represented in classical theory, defends itself against the attempt to make the unconscious conscious.
>
> (Bion [1962] 1991, pp. 15–16)

Here is a key part of the argument against symbolic decoding, and the point of departure from Freud: dream exists not so much as a reservoir of hidden meanings but as a 'contact barrier' and a safety barrier, allowing intercourse between conscious and unconscious. The contact barrier, made of breathable material, affords the dreamer an emotional experience.

This account of the functioning of mind links with a developmental story and is continuous with it, for the 'road from sense impressions to pictograms and waking dream thought is the same in a child as in an adult' (Ferro 2015a, p. 519). It is an inalienably interpersonal story; the presence of a 'dreaming' other is mandatory for the growth of mind, just as the presence of another is necessary for the baby's physical survival. If all goes well, the neonate's primitive, inchoate, psychotic terror and burgeoning aliveness can find a welcome, through the mother's or carer's capacity to 'dream', to intuit and imagine, these phenomena and thus make them bearable. She (or he or they) achieves this through a capacity to tolerate temporarily being in a paranoid-schizoid state themselves or, as Bion also put it, in a state of 'Negative Capability' (e.g. Bion 1970, p. 125). Feeling for and with the baby, the carer is a receptacle for the baby's projective identifications and able to live through the experience, thanks to a capacity for 'reverie', that is, the ability to accept an onslaught of projected, raw beta-elements and to 'alphabetise' or 're-dream' them, thanks to having developed her own working contact barrier and alpha-function. It is a process of mental/emotional digestion and metabolisation.

Reverie, 'a factor of the mother's alpha-function' (Bion [1962] 1991, p. 36), is the vehicle for 'a constant emotional exchange within the … couple, in which proto-emotions and proto-sensations – i.e. β elements – are evacuated and received by a mind capable of transforming them and returning them in elaborated form, together' – and this is crucial – 'with the method for performing this operation' (Ferro 2002, p. 54). The process of transformation itself is communicated and internalised. Transformation is also that of the channels of communication themselves. 'Psychical quality will be imparted to the channels of communication, the links with the child' (Ferro 2002, p. 54).

Container/contained

This is what Bion conceptualised as the construction of a 'container' (Bion [1962] 1991; [1963] 2018), an 'inner thinker unknown' (Ambrosiano and Gaburri [2009] 2018, p. 124), a mind capable of unconscious processing and of thought, feeling, reflection, and growth. It emerges out of the dream of another, for dreaming and thinking 'always have to do with a "we" … The singular being is always a plural being' (Civitarese and Ferro 2020, pp. 32–33). Dreaming and being dreamed lead, in the word of Bion's great commentator James Grotstein, to the birth of a 'dreamer who understands the dream'. Grotstein continued: 'The dreamer who dreams the dream is the ineffable subject of being' (Grotstein 2000, p. 46).

Expansion of the container must take place no faster than the baby, and the carer, can tolerate. In fact, two containers, the carer's and the baby's, grow together. This provides a conceptual model for a form of therapeutic practice 'that most closely corresponds to the idea that what grows and feeds the mind is the weaving of a sustainable meaning, or dreaming reality, just as in the nurturing relationship between mother and child' (Ferro and Civitarese 2015, p. xvi).

The purpose of analysis, in this Bionian thinking, is

to progressively add to the patient's set of tools that enable him to recognize, name, manage and metabolise emotions. This is a psychoanalysis that is more concerned with the tools for thinking and feeling than their content. Not that the content does not matter but if the piano is in good working order, it can produce all kinds of music depending on the individuality of the pianist.

(Ferro [2007] 2011, p. 105)

Bion's 'quantum leap' from Klein was what he would call a 'catastrophic change' (Bion [1970] 1984, etc.), and it was an expansion of the psychoanalytic container. Not interested in creating new conceptual models – 'he often says that there are already too many in psychoanalysis' – Bion, writes Ferro, provides us with new tools 'which enable us to think things we previously could not think ... to perform new operations or to acquire an awareness of the operations performed in the consulting room previously we did not have' (Ferro [2007] 2011, p. 50).

Waking dream thought

Dreaming, writes Ferro, is 'an ongoing activity of the mind that also operates in the waking state'. It is

an activity that unconsciously transforms our sensory and proto-emotional afferents into pictograms ... like having a kind of cameraman who is always on the job and then in the night dream a director/ editor takes over and carries out a kind of montage.[1]

Waking dream thought 'is surely the most important concept we owe to Bion' (Ferro [2002] 2005, p. 73).[2] It is the ever-changing sea on which our perceptual and emotional lives float, or 'the dough that transforms the sensorial and proto-emotional sensations into images, visual picto-grams that, put in sequence, form thought, and constitute … the "contact barrier"' (Ferro [2010] 2015, p. 73), which is in continuous formation without our awareness.

> This process … happens in every mind … We can-not know if other species do it, but I would say that our species is the one that does it the most; that is, we continually transform the sensory flow … of stimuli into a sequence of pictograms, into a dream sequence unknown to us. Our whole mental life depends on this dream sequence of pictograms that we do not know: we hang from this sequence of pictograms like our an-cestors hung from tree branches, assuming they did.
>
> (Ferro and Nicoli [2017] 2018, pp. 60–61)

For Ferro, 'waking dream thought' is the very stuff and motor of the analytic session.

Night dreams

Night dreams may be a sort of special case of this perpetual dreaming activity. Here the alpha-function may be 'work-ing on its own contents, performing a secondary level of elaboration on the α elements stored up during the day, which are then added to the immense store of unused α elements (the continuous source of stimuli represented by "undigested facts" – Bion 1962)', in a process of 'rumina-tion'. Alongside the 'apparatus for thinking thoughts', we might thus postulate an 'apparatus for dreaming dreams (Ferro [2002] 2013, p. 55)', in other words for putting unused alpha-elements to work. Dreams are the digestive 'viscera of the mind' (Ferro [2014] 2019).

Rather than a continuous recording, in real time, of current experience (waking dream thought's work), nocturnal dreams may involve 'a sort of meta-function … that, in the absence of stimuli, chooses certain elements by virtue of their pertinence'. Ferro compares this function to montage: the director (night dream) selects and assembles the images provided by the cameraman (waking dream) to create a dream, which will be one among an infinity of possible narrations (Ferro and Pizzuti 2001, paras 80–82). Grotstein also postulated an 'alpha-megafunction' (Grotstein, 2007, p. 271) that performs a 'second pressing or weaving of … material, eventually giving rise to dream images … the most digested elements which our apparatus for thinking thoughts is capable of producing' (Civitarese and Ferro 2013, pp. 200–201). Dreaming is 'a veritable matrix of the meaning of each individual's emotional life' (Ferro [1992] 1999, p. 107). The communication richest in alpha-elements, the dream is also 'a poem of the mind' (Ferro [2014] 2019, p. 37), and like a poem it does not require us to take 'the reverse path to dream work' and decodify it. Does 'There we are like in autumn on trees the leaves' require an interpretation, Ferro asks, or does it have 'an emotional resonance that puts us in touch with emotions linked to transience'? (Ferro [2010] 2015, p. 51).[3]

Failures of alpha

The alpha-function is

a kind of lithotripter [a machine for shattering gallstones ultrasonically] that deconstructs the symptom, crushing it into fragments that are sometimes invasive but nevertheless alive, [for] the reweaving of a new narrative ... how far these operations will go also depends on the type of resources patient and analyst have at their disposal.

(Ferro [2010] 2015, p. 69)

Indeed, to start an analysis means exposure for both patient and analyst to a traumatic situation, arising 'out of the disorder created by the mind in its continuous, albeit discreet, coupling' (Ferro [2007] 2011, p. 106).

For Ferro, psychopathology results from deficiencies or failures of alpha-function, which are the 'seeds of illness' (Ferro [2002] 2013). He agrees with Grotstein and Ogden: the factors determining illness or recovery 'coincide with the insufficiency or efficiency ... of the "dreaming ensemble"' (Grotstein, 2007, p. 50; Ferro 2009, p. 212).

In the most severe pathology, the alpha-function is simply lacking; there is 'deficiency in the formation of the visual pictogram' such that mind itself may fail to form. This situation is like that of 'a cine camera with no film stock; the basic frames out of which the eventual movie should be composed are lacking' (Ferro [2002] 2013, p. 2). In these 'unrepresented states', it may be necessary to dream the patient into life to construct a container from scratch. Thus, instead of dealing with 'Pandora's jars' of beta-elements, the analytic couple find themselves 'having to make the jars themselves, or indeed even needing to manufacture ... the necessary potter's tools' (Ferro [2007,] 2011 p. 106).

Then there is pathology due to the maldevelopment of container-contained and of the oscillation Ps ↔ D. Alpha-elements may have been formed, but the apparatus for processing them is deficient. The film is exposed, but then either it is not developed ... or the directorial function required to edit the vast number of frames shot – the Ps ↔ D work – is lacking, or else there is no place to keep the developed film (absence of the container-contained dynamic).

(Ferro [2002] 2013, p. 2)

In trauma, there is a quantitative excess of stimulation of beta-elements, like a storm of asteroids (Ferro 2016b, pp. 55–56). They are more than can be received or transformed, either by oneself or with another's help, into alpha-elements (Ferro [2002] 2013, p. 2; Ferro and Civitarese 2015, p. 20); there is a 'killer contained' and a failure or explosion of the container, an overwhelm of the analyst's receptivity and alpha-functioning, and of that of the field itself: 'the contained is more violent and explosive than the capacity for thinking it' (Ferro [2002] 2013, p. 31). The patient must mobilise extra defences to cope. In this situation, 'the mind that is supposed to receive and transform projects things into the mind that wants and needs to ... find a space and method to manage proto-emotions'. It is a situation of 'negative reverie' or 'Minus-R' (Ferro [2010] 2015, p. 98; Ferro and Civitarese 2015, p. 20). Ferro has also characterised it as the 'Negative Grid' or 'Minus-G' (Ferro 2023). A short animated film, *Dr Fish* (Ferro 2015), offers a nice illustration of the restoration of dream function that is required to re-establish the container when such disaster threatens.

Mariella, aged 60, suffers from insomnia and nightmares after a life of misfortunes. Her story could be told from several different vertices; Ferro prefers to see the lack of adequate alpha-function 'turning each proto-emotional state into a proliferation of monsters'. The commonest denominator among the experiences she recounts is cancer, 'unmanageable, uncontainable ... [destroying] all possibility of life' (Ferro [2010] 2015, p. 92). The monsters may also be 'undigested facts', lumps of partially processed beta-elements, or 'balpha'-elements, which must be powerfully evacuated, through splitting, disavowal, and so on. They can be projected 'like a film that separates, protects – and encloses – the patient inside a "bubble"', but also isolates him (Ferro [1999] 2006, p. 69, and see p. 47).[4]

Another defensive measure might be narcissism, in which others are treated as subsidiary functions (Ferro 2002, pp. 2–4). Or there is hallucination, in which fragments of beta-elements are expelled into the external world along with traces of ego and superego, thereby creating 'bizarre objects' (Bion ([1967] 1980) p. 47, etc.):

> Imagine a film show being interrupted by a mechanical fault which results in projecting not only bits of the film but also pieces of the crank, lenses and spools of the projector. The viewer has visual experiences which cannot be integrated into the sequence of images he was watching on the screen and the images become meaningless.

These need to be evacuated massively to avoid even worse situations, 'such as the confused dreamlike situations of the most dramatic psychotic experiences' (Ferro [1992] 1999, p. 102).

Ferro, wrote a colleague, knows 'how to "see" the apparatus for thinking in its element, and the α-function at the point when it is still in a nascent state in the encounter between the two parties of the analytic couple' (França 2013, p. xi).

He neither dismisses diagnostic categories nor enthusiastically embraces them. They are never a point of departure. How, asked an audience member in a seminar in São Paulo, does Ferro's approach work with perverse patients? Ferro responded: 'Can I say something terrible?' – as if risking a charge of heresy. 'It works by taking the good aspects of perversion and trying to understand, within the relationship, how the patient feels things' (Ferro 2013a, p. 127).

Alpha-function of the field

In trying to see how the patient sees things, the analyst is not merely being empathic. He/she is adopting a position, one among many other possible positions, within the field. Corrao referred to the field's 'gamma-function', the couple's capacity to step outside the subject/object dichotomy, and narrate, dream, think, and construct metaphors or myths that might give specific meaning to their common experience (Corrao 1986b). The field becomes 'a system dedicated to the transformation of sensory and emotional experiences into thoughts and meanings', the locus for a form of treatment 'centred on the transformations and development' of the field itself, 'rather than on individuals and contents' (Neri and Selvaggi 2006, p. 182, cited in Ferro and Civitarese 2015, pp. 7–8).

This is the field's own alpha-function. 'I often speak of the analyst's function. Perhaps it would be better to speak of the alpha-function of the field' and no longer 'refer to the alpha-function of the analyst or the beta-function of the patient, but … instead consider the situation in terms of the alpha-function … the beta-turbulences of the field' (Ferro and Pizzuti 2001, para 93). The field will contract the patient's illness, which 'must then be cured by returning a new and transformed type of functioning to the patient. This transformation will take place solely in the here-and-now of the session!' (Ferro 2015a, p. 523). And it will do so in a manner analogous to the reverie-based transformation of beta to alpha that allows the carer-baby couple to flourish.

The field concept 'extends and imparts rigour to the dream paradigm of the session'. It puts both Klein's concept of projective identification and Bion's 'waking dream thought' to work in the couple. Thus,

> There is no point in the field (whether an event, a memory, a dream, an enactment, a reverie, an association, an emotion, a sensation, or whatever) that is not touched by the 'electromagnetic waves' of the intersecting projective identifications of patient and analyst, and that does not correspond to the recordings made of it by their respective alpha functions.
>
> (Ferro and Civitarese 2015, p. 7)

Notes

1 In the post-war scientific climate within which Bion's thinking had been developing, the biologist J.Z. Young claimed: 'The brain of each one of us does literally create

his or her own world' (Young [1950] 1956, in Williams [1961] 2013).

2 Bion noted that nobody seemed to have taken any notice of this concept, 'a situation which persists today even though it is considered by some to be a concept capable of revolution-ising the whole of psychoanalytic technique' (Ferro [2014] 2019, p. 36).

3 'Soldati', a four-line poem of 1918 by Giuseppe Ungaretti (1888–1970).

4 These partially digested, projected beta-elements become linked to each other. They are literal 'regurgitations of dream material ... indicative of a ruminative state of mind' that continues until alpha-function can be restructured and the process of elaboration resumed, so that they can be transformed into alpha-elements (Ferro [1999] 2006, p. 70).

Chapter 3

Practice and theory

Characters

For Ferro the concept of the field is a point of difference with analysts such as Ogden, Grotstein, and Green. In Ferro's 'strong' concept of the field – 'understood not in the as yet somewhat simplified sense of Baranger and Baranger, but on a more complex level' – the internal groupings of both analyst and patient generate 'a group of presences, or characters – *affective holograms* in my parlance – resulting from the transformation in dreaming of what is said, acted out, and experienced by the minds of both analyst and patient' (Ferro 2015a, p. 513). These 'characters' are products and derivatives of the waking dream thought of both members of the couple; they are manifestations of the alpha-function of the field.

> It is as if Ogden's *analytic third* were diluted in a dream-like narration of the functioning of the two minds, which undertake the casting of the characters they need to breathe life into the particular dream that must be taken care of and – even before this – brought to life.
>
> (Ferro 2015a, p. 513)

DOI: 10.4324/9781003313311-4

Meaning is thus generated 'in the dimension of a *theatre of dreams*' (Ferro [1992] 1999, p. 107). The concept of characters is 'absolutely central to my thinking' (Ferro [2010] 2015, p. 136), and Ferro has been inventive in picturing this, drawing for example on the work of the Austrian/American magic realist painter Henry Koerner as a way of visualising a character-rich field that includes the analyst him/herself (Ferro 2023). Characters, each with its own unconscious motivations and emotional bonds (L, H, K), provide a highly accessible way of considering and adopting Bion's 'vertices' (Bion 1965, etc.). They are readily available, as they appear in the patient's narrations and the analyst's reveries, for both participants to identify with, move between, and experience in their changing interactions, reappearances, and disappearances, on the 'stage' of the analysis.

Characters

may find a great variety of stage sets and scripts but in the session they will speak of the workings of the mind of the field ... Each field will be a specific couple, as will the narratives and the hologram-like characters that come to life.

(Ferro 2013b, p. 141)

A character may come to occupy the site where a 'beta whirlwind' (Ferro [2014] 2019, p. 122) has appeared and is thus beginning to find its way to a narratable form. Characters must be allowed to enter the field 'with all the rights of citizens' (Ferro [2014] 2019, p. 122).

> Bion calls one of his books *Taming Wild Thoughts*, though in my opinion it is not about taming them but enabling us to live them, and if it is normal to read *Little Women* or *Good Wives* then it is normal to be able to watch *Apocalypto.*
>
> (Ferro 2015c, p. 183)

It is certainly not always possible to perform upon them 'operations of pure decoding' or to bring them into relation as if 'assembling ... a jigsaw puzzle; in these cases much has already been done and the characters are only waiting for the narrative to be edited' (Ferro 2015c, p. 184).

> Every patient comes to us with characters not 'in search of an Author' ... but with a confused mass, a nebula of proto-somites, proto-devils, proto-Mortimers... [Ferro is referring to Bion's *A Memoir of the Future*] that have rarely arrived at being characters. If we already had Characters we would already be in analysis that would be less of a challenge for our creative-inventive capacity (and by 'our' I mean the patient's and the analyst's).
>
> This is all the more true when a patient presents to us with 'zero characters' and these have to begin sprouting from a sort of desert.
>
> How do we enable boredom, silence, repetition or extreme stupidity to become *The Road, Crime and Punishment, The Silence of the Lambs, Anna Karenina?*
>
> There are analyses in which we can set off with characters who we imagine to be principal ones, and who may later on either confirm themselves as such or

leave the stage, while on the other hand new characters, unforeseen and unpredictable, may arrive.

With other analyses, in which trust is required, we can find ourselves in a Western where it is extremely hard to round up the herds that go running off in all directions, then lead them to the river and help them wade across towards thinkability.

(Ferro 2015c, p. 183)

Casting and narrative derivatives

Beta-elements, alphabetised into images and words and integrated into characters, contribute to the creation of 'narrative *plots*' (Ferro [1992] 1999, p. 107 and see Bezoari and Ferro 1990). Characters are chosen, and not chosen, through a process of 'casting' (Ferro [2014] 2019, p. 117), in the constant search for a character

> needed to say something that is urgent in the current relationship in the field … The dream thought co-formed in the field can be … given visibility, expression or narration through the characters that are called on stage as the case requires.
>
> (Ferro 2013b, pp. 140–141)

'It is as if rubber bands were being stretched between patient and analyst, like so many possible storylines to which, one by one, paper clips were gradually attached, and these are the casting the field makes of what was undetermined' (Ferro [2010] 2015, pp. 140–141), in other words, of what is in the process of beta-to-alpha transformation and seeking to find pictorial and verbal shape.

Thus, unlike in classical analysis, in which almost the entire list of protagonists is present from the beginning, 'as in an old-fashioned thriller', the development of a capacity for casting becomes one of the central aims of analysis, especially where the patient has a limited capacity for symbolization.

> Mute and inexpressible zones become a matrix for the generation of characters, whether animate or inanimate, present or past, and of stories that begin to make sense and become capable of narration, having previously lacked the possibility of expression. The casting will sometimes include film sets and places which must subsequently come to life.
>
> (Ferro 2009, p. 226)

Characters take their places in a scenario, a drama, that might belong within any number of possible genres. Ferro calls these scenarios 'narrative derivatives'. Through them waking dream thought makes itself known. They are sequences of pictograms and signs of a transformation from beta to alpha in progress. The 'choice and construction of an individual pictogram and of sequences of pictograms are extremely subjective. It is like one and the same subject painted by Degas, and then by Caravaggio, Monet, Chagall, Picasso, etc.' (Ferro and Civitarese 2015, p. 14).

> For instance, sensory/proto-emotional stimuli involving irritation, rage and finally the onset of a calmer mood could be transformed by the α-function into the following emotional pictograms

A stinging plant ------ A roaring lion ------ The sun appearing through clouds

This sequence of α-elements, which are in themselves inaccessible, could give rise to an infinite number of narrative derivatives in a wide variety of literary (or graphic or play-related) genres. For instance, it could become a chain of associations that might be expressed as follows

A childhood memory: 'When my father's friend announced at the table that he had bumped into me in the street during school hours, I was furious and would have liked to beat him up, but the unruffled expression on my father's face calmed me down.'

A scene from everyday life: 'Yesterday I saw some boys harassing an immigrant and I felt very irritated: I was about to tell them off, but then a policeman appeared and they ran away.'

A sexual scene: 'When Carla didn't want to make love, I got angry and was on the point of leaving and going back home, but then I discovered that she was having a surprise party and there were friends in the living room.'

A scene from a film: 'I remember a film sequence in which the hero takes a dim view of it when he sees his wife from behind kissing a man; he is about to attack her when he sees that she is in fact kissing their son, back from military service: my goodness how he had grown!'

An infinite number of examples could be adduced ...

(Ferro [2006] 2009, pp. 135–136)

A dream recounted in a session might also be a narrative derivative of the alpha-sequence belonging to the moment of recounting. So a narration of the scene above might be: 'I dreamt that I was stung in the dark by something I thought was a scorpion; I was furious with the person who had guaranteed me a safe journey but then discovered it was only a prickly plant' (Ferro [2006] 2009, p. 136).

The conversation in the consulting room often proceeds 'on a twofold level, in which the manifest text *metaphorises* the latent text of the unconscious/field dimension of the relationship—the invisible "electromagnetic waves" that establish it, exactly as in the case of play in the therapy of children' (Ferro and Civitarese 2015, pp. 24–25).

Narrative theory

This does not mean, however, that the 'fabula', understood by Ferro as the underlying pattern of the narration and of the mental exchanges between patient and analyst (Ferro [1999] 2006, pp. 117 and 129 n. 8), must immediately be spelled out. A patient relates: 'We are in a village, there is a tyre dealer who inflates tyres too much'. Ferro does not make the Kleinian interpretation, 'You are afraid that I'm filling you up too much with the things I say', which, apart from being already outdated, would mean 'the collapse of the field and a return to a highly relational situation' (I respond to you and you respond to me). In a field situation, he continues,

> we let these characters live and play with them … so we hand the story over to Nanni Moretti or Quentin Tarantino and see what movie comes out of it. We

cannot know beforehand, the best part is doing it together, building it: where are we going to end up today? 'Tonight we improvise', Pirandello would say.

(Ferro and Nicoli [2017] 2018, p. 93)

Plot and story line are not to be confused. For Ferro, the plot

bears the narrative load, but the beauty lies in the way the story line, the characters, the atmospheres, the places (and these are characters too) not only adorn the story but make it narratable and shareable outside the illusion of a neutral and sterile analysis, reduced to the skeleton of transference and countertransference.

What would become of Botticelli's Spring or Gilda if they were reduced to bone or skeleton? ... The beauty lies in the creation of semantic and narrative nests, in the invention of storylines and narremes which expand and proliferate under the germinating and creative impulse of that field to which the psychic lives of patient and analyst give life, in the Big Bang which generates the expanding narrative universe.

(Ferro 2017b, pp. 69–70)

The 'plot' might be an unconscious fantasy, a symptom, or the defences being used. 'But the leap towards the clinical and human experience which mutually engages analyst and patient has a thousand facets that are constantly in the making: this CREATIVITY is the motor, the "beauty" of analysis' (Ferro 2017b, p. 70).

Listen for the plot and elaborate the storyline: it is an approach that respects both the patient's 'inalienable right ...to think that when she speaks of her husband she is "really" talking about her husband' (Ferro [2010] 2015, p. 130), and 'the fabric of a session', typically 'a dance between narratives of a visual character – reveries, metaphors, dreams' (Ferro [2014] 2019, p. 25).

The instruments at the analyst's disposal include the investigations of semiotics and narratology (Ferro [2002] 2013, p. 60).[1] They help conceptualise the field itself, all the elements of which are 'structured as a differential system in which each term is defined in relation to the others in a process of constant, mutual cross-reference', an observation with echoes of de Saussure's conception of the structure of language, Lacan's of the system of signifiers in the unconscious, or Derrida's of the text. Perhaps only chaos theory, Civitarese and Ferro note, 'could offer a really effective representation of the dynamism of the field', modelling 'complex vectorial manifestations that give rise to turbulence, catastrophic points, and ultimately changes of state' (Civitarese and Ferro 2013, p. 195).

The philosophy of Jacques Derrida has certainly informed Ferro's thinking, in so far as Derrida's concept of deconstruction 'is *not* an interpretation that dissects the text, as it is often misunderstood, but a reading that opens the way to a huge number of possibilities that are only seemingly arbitrary' (Ferro and Civitarese 2015, pp. 67–68, n. 2). The inherent polysemy of the text, indeed of every word, works against interpretative closure (IJP Open 2021, p. 12).

The works of Umberto Eco have also been a fundamental stimulus, starting from *The Open Work* (Eco [1962 etc.] 1989), which put forward the idea of the text as a co-construction and fed into a view of the analytic session too as something to be read from a bi-personal perspective (IJP Open 2021, p. 12). Eco's influence is explicit in the title of Ferro's book *La psicoanalisi come opera aperta* (Ferro 2000c, untranslated).

The idea of 'interpretive cooperation' between analyst and patient in relation to the text that comes into being between them parallels the collaboration, as Eco understood it, between reader and literary text in the production of meaning (Eco 1979; Ferro [1999] 2006, p. 91). Eco developed the concept of the 'inferential stroll' (Eco 1979, p. 118), in which the reader goes outside the text 'to re-enter it laden with intertextual booty', plundered from her experiences of life or from other 'free and disengaged' readings (IJP Open 2021, pp. 12–13).

But there are, Ferro notes, differences between the literary character, which tends towards a degree of objective fixity, and the psychoanalytic character, which is 'articulated progressively by way of the dialogic and projective interaction patient and analyst … a dynamic entity that is never completely defined, of twofold paternity, subject to constant additions and modifications' (Ferro [1999] 2006, p. 91). Certain literature can, however, give us a very vivid sense of what meeting psychoanalytic characters, and participating in their generation, can involve.

The protagonists in Joyce's *Finnegans Wake* (1939), one of Ferro's favourite books, 'do not retain their identities throughout the novel' (unlike those in *Ulysses*). 'H. C. E.', the publican Humphrey Chimpden Earwicker, also becomes 'Here Comes Everybody', 'everybody through all time, from Adam to Noah, Cromwell, Caesar, Napoleon, Wellington and an infinite number of other characters of the story and of legend'. The same applies to his wife Anna Livia Plurabelle. 'There is a continuous metamorphosis of characters who transmute from one to another in a history in the throes of constant transformation' (Ferro [1999] 2006, p. 90).

Like Joyce's approach in *Finnegans Wake*,

the approach to psychoanalytic narration is based on the criterion of maximum openness, in such a way that the analyst (as well as the patient) allows himself to roam freely between the 'possible worlds' suggested by the emotional context of the moment, at the same time undertaking, outside the text, all the inferential walks that promise to be pleasurable and productive … without either magnifying or a priori anaesthetising any possible channel of sense … an important element of this process is the pleasure derived by analyst and patient alike from the interpretive activity: the patient gives up his purely passive role, and participates in the more or less unconscious search for *proportio* that presses for the unification of the words of the text and the elements of reality in an interplay of harmonious relations.

(Ferro [1999] 2006, p. 91)

For even more than in literary narration, 'characters in psychoanalytic narration prove to be the fundamental element that determines and regulates textual cohesion and coherence, thus making the narration itself legible' (Ferro [1999] 2006, p. 91). So it is not correct to claim, with Richard Rorty (1989), or in line with deconstructivist theses

(De Man, Derrida, Miller, Culler, etc.) 'which allow the reader to produce "drifts" with increasing levels of meaning … to the point of uncontrolled or unlimited readings', that any reading of a text is legitimate. For Eco (1990), what matters is less the intention of the reader than the intention of the work, the structure of which sanctions a particular reading but stands in the way of another. The preferential guidelines for one's reading are to be sought in the text, just as, for the analyst, in 'the emotional and relational context of the session', and certainly not in the analyst's favourite analytic categories (Ferro [1999] 2006, p. 91).

Narratological concepts such as the 'limit of interpretation' and 'limit of the opening of possible worlds' can thus 'provide significant assistance in setting boundaries' (Ferro 2005, p. 93) – in orienting oneself in the multiverse of the field (Ferro 2005, p. 93, and see Ferro 2009, p. 218, Eco [1979] 1981, and Pavell 1976). This is essential for the patient's introjection of the 'analytic function'.

> At a certain point, the shared narration is superseded by the active, stabilized function of an internal narrator able to confer a name, meaning and history on what had previously been exerting pressure in the form of emotional sensory 'lumps'.
>
> (Ferro [2002] 2013, p. 61)

Mourning is required for every other possible interpretation (or over-interpretation): a move away from Negative Capability, that special form of the paranoid-schizoid, to the depressive position. Ferro turns to a passage in another favourite novel, Denis Diderot's *Jacques le fataliste* (1796), in which Diderot announces to the reader that he does not intend to pursue a possible new storyline that has just arisen with the appearance of a new character. 'In other words, the author is forgoing all the possible stories *in favour of the story that is pressing to be told*, which involves the loss of other narrative possibilities'. There is a constant oscillation between an opening and closing of sense, as with Bion's PS ↔ D, and which, as Diderot knew (he gave his novel three alternative endings), never reaches stasis (Ferro [1999] 2006, pp. 7–9).

There is finally the question of lies (to which we shall be returning). Eco conceived of semiotics itself as a theory of lying:

> A sign is everything which can be taken as significantly substituting for something else. This something else does not necessarily have to exist or to actually be somewhere at the moment in which a sign stands in for it. Thus semiotics is in principle the discipline studying everything which can be used in order to lie. If something cannot be used to tell a lie, conversely it cannot be used to tell the truth: it cannot in fact be used 'to tell' at all.
>
> (Eco 1976, p. 7)

'Truth without a handle of lies', said Ferro,

> would look like a hot frying pan that some one asked us to hold, while inside it fries are sizzling in steaming oil and the temperature is unapproachable: we need that handle of lies in order to pick up the pan and the truth

(and the excellent fries that truth offers us). Our species
cannot tolerate the harsh, hard impact with reality.
(Ferro and Nicoli [2017] 2018, pp. 138–139. See too
Ferro 2009, p. 211)

Forms of attention: Negative Capability and theoretical models

Bion liked to invoke what Keats famously called 'Negative Capability' (e.g. Bion 1970, p. 125): 'that is when man is capable of being in uncertainties, Mysteries, doubts, without any irritable reaching after fact and reason' (Keats 1958, vol. 1, p. 193). Thanks to Bion, the phrase has come to signify analytic receptivity in all its dimensions, including the abstinent, open-minded attitude Freud recommended when he wrote of 'free floating' or 'evenly suspended' attention (Freud [1912] 1953–64). Its foundational value for practice is something on which all analytic schools would agree. At the same time, the analyst's listening, however radically open, will also be informed and inflected by her particular theoretical orientation and assumptions.

Ferro has schematised the main analytic models, together with the listening vertices and healing factors they suggest (a difficult task, he notes, because there are so many of them), with particular regard to the status each gives 'reality' (Ferro 2013b, p. 114), and the degree of their emphasis on historical reconstruction and on making the unconscious conscious (Ferro 2009, p. 210). The importance given to analysing defences might be another fault line.

The Freudian model, concerned with the childhood determinants of adult neurosis, looks at historical events and traumas, and the vicissitudes and genealogies of the drives, and aims to remove the veil of repression. The second, Kleinian model looks at early fantasy life and unconscious fantasies and the distortions they cause, together with 'vicissitudes with the primary object, splits and integrations, the PS and D movement, the death instinct and the weight of envy' (Ferro 2013b, pp. 114–115).

The third, Bion-inspired model, interested in 'the development of tools for feeling, dreaming and thinking', looks with only half an eye at most at content. It is more concerned with 'the development of the way the mind works and the "qualities" the mind has that can be developed on the way towards relative mental health'. This path, Ferro adds, involves suffering and pain, but also holds out the prospect of the pleasure to be found in knowledge and adventure.

'Post-Bionian', 'post-field' theory marries 'what has been "worked out" by writers such as Ogden and Grotstein with what has been "worked out" by writers such as Baranger and Corrao … the analytic session appears as a dream of two minds where stories from different places and times … arrive, diffract and overlap', with the analyst himself a locus in the field (Ferro 2013b, pp. 114–115, and see Ferro ([1992] 1999. pp. 2–9).

A leap is made in those models where the person is considered a character of the session … If in earlier models people were flesh and blood, real, historical, and then become internal objects, now they are holographic images of a hidden dream of the field that comes to life through projective identifications that must find meaning … later models see as a healing factor the development of tools that are able to fulfil a narrative, dream-like, micro-mythopoeic function.

(Ferro 2013b, pp. 140–141)

Ferro also suggests a 'possible middle way', in which all the above, along with other dialects and scenarios, are available to inform the analyst's listening. All can become vehicles for the development of the container and of alpha-function, 'even if this takes place without analyst and patient being aware of it' (Ferro 2009, p. 210). Learning to listen and to attend is inherently pleasurable, Civitarese and Ferro have written. They note the view of the Russian psychologists Vigotsky and Lurija: 'the prime function of language is not so much to communicate as to monitor attention' (Civitarese and Ferro 2020, p. 85).

Dream listening

Asked what qualities the analyst needs, Ferro's 'off-the-cuff' answer was 'benevolence, trust in his method, the ability to blind himself to any reality that is not that of the consulting room' (Ferro [2014] 2019, p. 34). 'The analyst's faith in the method, his reveries, intuition, negative capability, and *capacity to listen to the hidden recesses of language* are the fertilizers that will allow the desert to bloom' (Ferro 2009, p. 226).

Since the field is a 'waking dream', it requires an oneiric form of listening, so that the process of dreaming into life can be furthered, and proto-emotions and proto-characters can 'gradually acquire depth, colour and three-dimensionality' (Ferro [2010] 2015, pp. 140–141). For Bion, the unconscious is the seat of the 'psychoanalytic function of the personality': its capacity to transform itself. So 'one must make the conscious unconscious: that is, render conscious experience available for the unconscious work of the dream' (Ferro [2010] 2015, p. 73). The analyst's task is thus a reversal of Freud. It is to 'unconscious' or 'unconsciate', *inconsciare*, the verb replacing the noun 'the better to reflect processuality and becoming' (Ferro and Civitarese 2015, p. xv).

The analyst's first contribution to the session is to mourn external reality (Ferro 2016b, p. 57, citing the Sicilian analyst Aldo Costa), and discover 'the historicity of the present' (Ferro and Civitarese 2015, p. xiv). The 'vertex towards which the analyst orientates himself' is thus 'a kind of listening that deconstructs, de-concretizes and re-dreams the patient's communications' (Ferro [2010] 2015, p. 73). It involves finding ways not of ignoring but of bracketing off the 'reality' of the patient's narratives, of 'keeping the cinema lights off'.

> [B]lindness to all external reality allows us to see scenes in the consulting room that the glare of external reality would obliterate … There are no external scenes if we make it dark all around us: the dramatization of the analytic scene takes on density, life and body, and so we can have a truly transformative function within it … In short, the consulting room becomes the stage where the whole of Shakespeare, Pirandello, Molière, Ibsen and the rest come to life in an infinity of affective storylines which lose substance and vitality if we let in

the light from outside … in a cinema, you need to keep the emergency lights turned on, but it has to be dark. We allow life and lights in the consulting room if we make it completely dark outside.

Of course, this does not mean taking substance away from historical or existential reality, but allowing it to become embodied there, in the only place where it can be transformed, and if 'my boyfriend won't answer his phone' to live through the pain of this with the patient, knowing that it is we ourselves who have not answered, and that it would be too simple to interpret it. First, we must 'answer'.

Thinking about the internal object that does not answer – the mother who has not answered in the past – stops the drama coming fully to life in the consulting room; whereas, if we are aware and the patient is not, we will continue to be called the 'boyfriend', and the drama will stay alive.

(Ferro [2014] 2019, pp. 34–35)

At first sight paradoxically perhaps, giving too much attention to the patient's history and objective reality risks neglecting his suffering. 'The result is a kind of operational thinking about facts and memories-as-facts, of rationalizations lacking in genuine affective involvement'. The analyst feels mainly sympathy, which is defensive in nature; actually he is abdicating responsibility. He should, instead, 'be receptive, listening on the basis of fundamental acceptance of the notions of unconscious communication between minds and the dream paradigm' (Ferro and Civitarese 2016, p. 311).

For Ferro, a kind of 'magic philter' is needed, and the more 'real' 'dramatic' or 'objective' the situation the patient narrates, the more the analyst is at risk of losing the magic philter (Ferro and Basile [2009] 2018, p. 11).

A little trick to aid deconstruction might therefore be to premise each communication by the patient with the enzyme – the word comes to me almost automatically – 'I had a dream', and to open up this dream by furnishing it with unexpected 'objects' rather than picking up on the concreteness of the communication.

(Ferro [2010] 2015, p. 14)

As Proust writes in 'The Captive', … 'everything is capable of transposition'. There is no fact, event, memory, account of a dream, and the like, that cannot stand for something else. If we accept the suggestion … that we should precede everything the patient says (as well as everything that we say) with the words 'I dreamt that …,' in order to recover an 'internal setting' (Civitarese [2010] 2013), the frame of reference is immediately shifted, thus saving his (or our) words from running aground on a realism lacking in personal significance, reopening the way to the play of meaning, and revealing to the patient (and to ourselves) the path toward the resumption of dreaming one's interrupted or undreamt dreams—i.e. one's very existence (Ogden 2005).

(Ferro and Civitarese 2015, pp. 25–26)

Analysis is the setting for a 'transformation in dream' (Ferro 2018b, pp. 49–50). What happens in the session is '"virtual", "in-between", existing in a kind of "no man's land" between external and internal reality, provided that the analyst, patient and setting are imbued with sufficient life and vitality' (Ferro [2006] 2009, p. 158).

It might help, in trying to appreciate this oneiric way of thinking, to locate it in the context of a long Italian tradition, as represented, for example, by Federico Fellini, some of whose dream drawings are reproduced in Ferro's *Torments of the Soul* ([2010] 2015, and Fellini [2007] 2008). Having, around 1960, moved away from his Neo-Realist roots (Kezich [2002] 2007, p. 227), Fellini found greater emotional resonance and truth in the dream-like quality, hovering between conscious and unconscious, and dream and waking reality, for which his later films are famous. 'It is not memory that dominates my films ...', he said. 'It seems to me that I have invented almost everything: childhood, character, nostalgias, dreams, memories, for the pleasure of being able to recount them' (Fellini 1980).

Or by Luigi Pirandello, in whose *Six Characters in Search of an Author* a character asks:

> why would you want to ruin, in the name of a commonplace sense of truth [una verità volgare, di fatto], this miracle of a reality that is born, evoked, attracted and formed by the stage itself and which has more right to live here than all of you, because it is much truer than you?
>
> (Pirandello [1921] 1995, p. 39)

Or by the Romantic poet Giacomo Leopardi, for whom, in 1828, the world and its objects were also 'in a certain respect double'.

A sensitive and imaginative man, who lives, as I have done for so long, continually feeling and imagining … will see a tower, a landscape; with his ears he will hear the sound of a bell; and at the same time with his imagination he will see another tower, another landscape, he will hear another sound. The whole beauty and pleasure of things lies in this second kind of objects. Sad is that life (and yet life is generally so) which sees, hears, feels only simple objects, only those objects perceived by the eyes, the ears, and the other senses.

(Leopardi 2015, pp. 1991–1992)

The model of the dream-field is Negative Capability really taken to heart. It requires the analyst to bear 'to wait for meaning to define itself', in a paranoid-schizoid state of uncertainty or confusion in which 'every hypothesis of meaning that we make, every metaphor that we use, must be quickly abandoned so that we can put ourselves in a state of mind that is open to the new and unpredictable' (Ferro [2010] 2015, p. 73). This does indeed mean abandonment of 'memory and desire', as Bion recommended (Bion [1967] 1988).

'How inadequate "doubt" is to express a state of extreme uncertainty', wrote James Joyce's secretary and Bion's former patient Samuel Beckett. In his work on what became *Finnegans Wake*, Joyce replaced the word 'doubt' with 'twosome twiminds' (Beckett 1929, pp. 10–11), and one is, of course, in at least two minds in the co-created field: the field concept underlines the importance of maintaining a state of radical doubt and openness, in which the analyst must be prepared to tolerate and allow the work of an 'unconscious' that he cannot even call his own.

Reverie

When the analyst is with the patient, wrote Ferro, 'he forms other pictograms generated by listening to the narrative derivatives of the patient with the addition of the alphabetization of shares of the patient's beta they had not transformed' (Ferro [2010] 2015, pp. 140–141). In other words, he is active in the process of alphabetisation, unconsciously, semi-consciously, and consciously. Reverie is among instruments that 'constantly widen the field to whose exploration they are applied' (Ferro [1992] 1999, p. 98).

It is a 'breathing of the mind' (Civitarese 2023, p. 44) and food for the mind, 'an ongoing *baseline activity* ... the way in which his mind constantly receives, metabolises and transforms everything that reaches him from the patient in the form of verbal, preverbal and non-verbal communication'. It is 'the cornerstone of our mental life, and our psychic health, illness or suffering is determined by its functional or dysfunctional status' (Ferro [2006] 2009, p. 1).[2] For the reformed Kleinian Ferro, its 'indispensible engine' is a *'baseline projective identification'*, which 'manifests itself in explicit and meaningful form – usually, but of course not exclusively, on the visual level' (Ferro [2006] 2009, p. 1).

A reverie is 'an image ... that is created in the mind – spontaneously and not to order'. It is 'like a small fragment of a dream triggered by situations permeated with projective identifications or ... beta elements' (Ferro and Civitarese 2015, p. 22). It can 'take a variety of forms: a flash when it is instantaneous, a feature film when it arises out of a connection between different moments of reverie' (Ferro [2014] 2019, p. 58). Its 'difficulty lies in organising it in pertinent, explanatory communication' (Ferro and Civitarese 2015, p. 22).

It is a 'continual activity', but

> only a reverie in a strict sense when, during a session, while I'm building without knowing a series of pictograms … at one point one of these pictograms, instead of remaining hidden from myself, becomes something with which I get into contact.
>
> (Ferro and Nicoli [2017] 2018, p. 75)

Its products, being unconscious, are not only unbidden but can be very unwelcome. Because the concept is at risk of 'meaning anything and everything', Ferro has come to favour a restrictive view of it. Something presents itself to the analyst at work 'insistently and annoyingly'; 'real phenomena of reverie' are 'insistent and grating' (Ferro and Nicoli [2017] 2018, p. 75, and Ferro [2010] 2015, p. 105). It imposes itself, even seeming to interfere with a receptive, listening state of mind. It usually has a bearing on the present state of the analytic situation and can lead to its deepening and expansion. For example, the image of a ship in a bottle started coming to Ferro's mind. He tried driving it away, but it kept returning, and only when he accepted it was he able to reflect and realize for the first time that he and the patient were in an impasse (Ferro and Nicoli [2017] 2018, p. 74).

Reverie, metaphor, free association, countertransference

Reverie draws on unconscious material. It is 'characterised by direct contact with the pictogram that constitutes the waking dream thought'. It can therefore be thought about as different and 'upstream' from both metaphor and free association, the latter a widening of a narration that is already underway (Civitarese and Ferro 2013, p. 206).

Reverie certainly creates space for a new metaphor to emerge. In the situation of impasse revealed by the the ship in a bottle, Ferro was able to draw on his knowledge of literature and say to the patient: 'You and I seem to be utterly becalmed, like Conrad's description of a ship when there is no wind' (Ferro and Nicoli [2017] 2018, p. 74). 'In an analytic session, we constantly alternate between metaphor and reverie' (Ferro and Melícias 2016, p. 514).

Reverie may even be the essential precondition for a truly 'living', unforced metaphor, that is, not one 'taken from an encyclopaedia [but] created there, in that place, for the first time' (Civitarese and Ferro 2013, pp. 205–206). Distinctions between reverie and metaphor can become blurred (the 'ship in a bottle' is already on the way to becoming a metaphor). Both are 'forms of intuition'. They are 'successful dreams', like 'fragments of poetry'. They are 'psychic productions that restore body to mind and mind to body'. They are 'the most profound form of thought of which we are capable', products of 'the psychoanalytic function of the personality that is constantly working to find, or rediscover, a basic psychosomatic integration' (Ferro and Civitarese 2015, p. 94).

Visual/verbal pictures that speak to profound interpersonal attunement, they can be transformational in themselves. Ferro, anxious about a coming train journey in the U.S., consulted a close friend, Anna Ferruta, who responded by saying '3.10 to Yuma' (referring to the films of 1957 and 2007). This immediately reminded Ferro of 'Westerns, the childhood roots of my childhood fears, the fear of being attacked in the wilderness', and his anxieties abated. '[I]f anxiety, anguish, unthought fragments of proto-emotions are transformed into a coherent and consistent image, this results in the feeling of peace and emotional relief' (Ferro [2010] 2015, p. 51).

Perhaps Ferruta's '3.10 to Yuma' could also be considered a free association. Indeed, 'an association may share the nature of a reverie' (Ferro and Civitarese 2015, p. 22). But Ferro also makes an important theoretical distinction. The concept of free association rests on Freud's theory of the unconscious as a reservoir of the repressed, the free associative method and 'fundamental rule' being what is required to access its depths and bring its contents to the shore of consciousness. But, says Ferro,

> what we have always mistaken for free associations are obligated associations stemming from that film of waking dream thought that is taking shape in our minds without us knowing it … given a situation, given a patient, given an analyst, then they have to make that specific dream, they are not free at all.
>
> (Ferro and Nicoli [2017] 2018, p. 60)

'Countertransference' is another case in point.

There is a myth that the analyst can always discover what is going on in the session by 'using' his own countertransference as a pointer. Bion exploded this myth in a few simple words when he stated that one of the founding characteristics of countertransference

is that it is *unconscious*, and thus the analyst cannot
make any use of it, since he does not know what it is
(Bion 1980).

(Bezoari and Ferro 1992a, p. 61)

Furthermore, the classical concepts of transference and
countertransference 'presuppose a configuration in which
analysand and analyst "face each other" as two positive,
pure, complete, and separate subjectivities, each some-
how totally "external" to the other' (Ferro and Civitarese
2015, p. 5). It makes better sense to see the ensemble of
the analyst's emotions, feelings, and experiences not so
much as expressions of 'countertransference' as of 'the
work the analyst is doing in the moment to welcome and
transform the patient's projective identifications' (Ferro
and Pizzuti 2001, para 87).

Finally, within the field paradigm, attention formerly
devoted to observing the patient's communications and
the countertransference now becomes attention to the figures taking shape in the field: 'all the "obscure" emotional
events that used to be picked up by the countertransference are now usually—before activating countertransference manifestations—signalled by the field, provided that
the analyst is able to listen to the narrations of the session
as forming part of the current field' (Ferro [1999] 2006,
p. 100).

Elaboration and interpretation

By means of 'oneiric' listening, helped by a magic philter
(or perhaps 'filter' too), the analyst builds without knowing a series of pictograms (Ferro and Nicoli [2017]

2018, p. 75), allowing unconscious to communicate with unconscious.

The analyst's task is now to further the alpha-function of the field through a process of 'elaborating' the narratives and characters it is producing. This might involve 'inferential strolling' (Eco 1979), a temporary departure of the analyst's mind from the text of the session, a departure which should in optimal conditions (the adequate functioning of the analyst's mind) be unconsciously driven. It is 'a way of withdrawing from the tyranny and fascination of the text itself … in order to elaborate original readings' and in this way to colour and fertilise the text through 'the unique way in which the patient's words meet the analyst's own life experiences, professional experiences, and moods in order to conceive something original'. What is produced must then be subjected to a selection, which enables the analyst to enlighten the analysand and offer him something which may be of use to him (IJP Open 2021, pp. 12–13).

Elaboration – *elaborazione* – is both what the alpha-functioning field invites and the means through which the field becomes an expanding universe and container. The Italian word can mean 'elaboration', 'processing', 'development', 'formulation', or 'digestion'; *elaborazioni* for Ferro will typically take the form of 'unsaturated' verbal touches, coloured by what is emerging 'live' through the work of the analyst's and the field's alpha function. They will be responses to what is developing, like, as I have suggested elsewhere (Snell 2021), those of a painter in front of the canvas, who is focussed, like Cézanne, on registering his 'sensations' in an 'abstracted' way;

he temporarily brackets off the 'reality' of the subject, in other words what he may think he already knows or understands. Such an artist is unconcerned with preconceived notions of 'likeness' or truth, derived perhaps from photographs or, in the analyst's case, literal-mindedness or diagnostic expertise.

So, said Bion: 'get out your colours!'. Bion was himself a landscape painter. 'What sort of artist are you?' he asked his audience of analysts in Paris in 1978; 'a great many analysts don't really know what sort of artists they are'. 'So although your tendency may be to say you don't paint, I say you do. Therefore, get out your colours' (Bion [1978] 2019).

> I become aware of the qualities of my verbal painting, of the shading of tones, of certain characteristics of my colours, and I 'learn to paint' from the patient who teaches me to make paintings which correspond increasingly to what she feels and experiences in the session. But the patient also 'learns to paint' from me, and I teach her how to proceed from a purely chromatic depiction of sensations to a figurative technique, which entails the recognition and description of her own feelings and emotions.
>
> (Ferro [1992] 1999, p. 48)

The process of 'elaboration' of the field and its characters and narratives involves 'answering' (Ferro [2014] 2019, p. 35). Prematurely 'saturated' interpretations, tripartite interpretations as recommended by Strachey, or transference interpretations as promulgated by Klein, can bring about a closure, when the aim is to keep the field open for further joint elaboration. 'I don't think that there is a need, moment by moment, to interpret the transformations that happen in the session. It's like making soufflé: if you open the oven door too soon, it collapses' (Ferro 2013, p. 67). 'As analysts we do not think enough of the side effects of our interpretations', Ferro has said, and we too often dismiss them as 'negative therapeutic reaction' or 'psychotic transference'. 'We must learn to speak with the patient in such a way as to give him the greatest number of growth factors and the smallest number of side effects' (Ferro 2013a, p. 55).[3]

Metaphors are particularly valuable colours in the box, forms of unsaturated intervention that can help us see things 'as children do; and children of course produce highly original metaphors'. They make it possible

> to see again with new eyes, a capacity possessed by poets in greater measure than anyone else. For this reason, it is indeed the case that 'metaphors can be the ghosts of ideas waiting to be born' (Bion, 1977, p. 418).
>
> (Civitarese and Ferro 2013, p. 198)

The analyst's 'touches' might be very tentative, and/or they might be spontaneous, visceral, and humorous:

> When conducting supervision groups … I increasingly find myself reversing the dictum 'think before you speak' into 'speak before you think', because one can then make contact with the dream-like functioning of the mind, which can create more connexions and meanings than any 'reasoning.'
>
> (Ferro [2002] 2013, p. 9)

Perhaps, we can hear echoes of Leopardi again:

> this might well be the source of great art, and of great effect, obtaining that vagueness and uncertainty, which belongs especially to poetry, and awakening images whose reason is not obvious, but almost hidden, and such that they seem accidental and not sought after by the poet in any way, but as though inspired by something invisible and incomprehensible and by that ineffable wavering of the poet who … does not know exactly how to express what he feels, except in a vague and uncertain way, and it is therefore perfectly natural that the images awakened by his words appear to be accidental.
>
> (Leopardi 2015, p. 29)

'Minute, refined analysis is not the same as seeing at a glance and never discovers a major part of nature', said Leopardi (Leopardi 2015, p. 831). 'I love it when I find an answer in two seconds!', said Ferro (Ferro and Nicoli [2017] 2018, p. 8).

A young woman comes to be interviewed by Ferro for a place at a school of psychotherapy and, as she enters the room, announces in ringing tones,

> 'I am Emilia.' Just as she is sitting down I say to her, 'And so tell me about Romagna!' [Ferro is playing on the name of the province of Emilia-Romagna]. She immediately gets it: he is not interested in what she already knows about herself but in all those things she doesn't really know, things that are 'confused and obscure'.

Needless to say, she is offered a place (Ferro [2014] 2019, p. 67).

With an aggressive, terrifying patient, there is a climate of fear and violence. One day,

> not knowing what else to do… I said 'With you I feel like I'm in one of those movie scenes in the Wild West, when a glass falls and everybody in the saloon pulls out a gun and starts shooting'. He made a huge smile and from there on we started talking through westerns, and went along this road for some time … it is very different from saying 'Inside you there is a destructive part etc …'.
>
> (Ferro 2013a, pp. 153–154)

Ferro's motto, borrowed from Pirandello, is 'Tonight We Improvise' (Ferro 2015a, p. 524): there are many possible levels and modes of interpretation, with different degrees of usefulness, depending on the moment and circumstances.

A 'character' might typically be a kind of narrative 'ball' (like a ball of yarn) waiting to be woven by analyst and patient. If that ball, Ferro wrote, were to be called 'Mario' (the character's name) and referred to a 'lava lump' of violence and uncontainability, 'this would have to be deconstructed and narrated in a way that can be "worn" by the patient'.

Interventions likely to be rejected by the patient might include:

> 'Mario is the part of you that …' or 'Mario enters the scene when …' and even 'Mario is the function that

…' Then there are intermediate forms such as 'Mario has perhaps similar features to you when …' or 'Mario reminds you of something about yourself'.

In a more telling narrative approach, Mario the ball of yarn might be deconstructed into the threads that compose him, and then re-woven:

'It would seem that Mario is jealous of Caterina when …' thus introduces the yellow thread of jealousy or 'what angers Mario …' introduces the red thread of anger, and so on. There is no need to go so far as an exhaustive interpretation; it is enough to disentangle the 'Mario ball of yarn' and to re-weave it with a pattern and a design that the patient can understand and take on board.

(Ferro [2007] 2011, pp. 99–100)

This is not to preclude the occasional exhaustive interpretation: 'indeed at some point there must be one' (ibid.). A 'point of urgency' – as discussed by Pichon-Rivière – will arrive, 'a moment in the functioning of the field when the structure of the dialogue and the underlying structure (the basic unconscious fantasy of the field) can come together and give rise to an insight' (Sabbadini and Ferro 2010, p. 421). But as a general approach, what applies to Mario also applies to any 'ball of yarn' or narrative that takes its place in the field, in any way or any form (Ferro [2007] 2011, pp. 99–100). It is a nice coincidence that in English 'yarn' also means 'story'.

Ferro helps his patient in the way a sensitive adult might help a frightened child by showing her a picture book: 'the rabbit is frightened when he sees the farmer

…' The hotter the emotional magma, the more productive a playful narration, rather than a direct confrontation, can be. Discussing in a supervision the case of a patient with a violent older brother, Ferro finds a dream 'in which the patient is finally able to "spray shit" quite wonderful'.

> Had I been there and had it been a good day with the right emotional climate and atmosphere, I may well have intervened by saying lightheartedly: 'Welcome, Bill (using the older brother's name), we've been expecting for you for a long time!' In other words, a simple way of expressing that a depressed and inhibited mode of functioning had finally shown its face.
>
> (Ferro 2016b, p. 56)

Another patient, after several months of analysis, describes a dream in which,

> expecting to be sent very detailed e-mails from me, in fact all he receives are some very short e-mails with attachments containing pictures and small stories. I offer a reading of the dream (which I later thought of as dictated by my superego): I did not provide him with what he expected to receive. 'On the contrary,' he says, 'in this room I feel like a balloon, and the images, the short stories you tell me are like brief shoves given to the balloon as it floats around the room, always discovering new points of view.'
>
> (Ferro [2007] 2011, p. 29)

Psychoanalysis, Ferro notes, 'used to have a horror of the analyst infecting the patient, the pollution that would ensue if the threshold of analytic neutrality were lowered; the analyst was not allowed to introduce any phantasies or to use metaphors or reverie'. This leaves out of account the fact that 'neutrality' belongs to the fabric of the field 'just like any other emotional colouring' (Ferro [2007] 2011, p. 101).

'I think reparative activity is essential … when it involves the grafting on of extra pieces, provided they come into being in the field and in the dream thought of the analyst' (Ferro [2007] 2011, p. 101).

Supervision and the Global Positioning System (GPS)

Attempting to attune to the patient, the analyst is guided in her/his activity by signals, or supervision, from the field, as if by a sort of SatNav or GPS. For the patient is always (also) narrating the dream level of the analytic couple's functioning: 'what a patient says after an interpretation is also a dream made about the interpretation: the characters that appear are therefore relevant to the way in which the patient felt the interpretation' (Ferro [2010] 2015, p. 139). The patient's response to an interpretation can also be a signal of the movement of the field, and this has been one of Ferro's principles from early on.

When we speak of intimacy, we do not mean something akin to fusionality, but, rather, a condition in which the interpretation of what is going on in the field remains a *fil rouge* in the analyst's mind – a real Ariadne's thread that helps him not to lose his way.

(Bezoari and Ferro 1992a, p. 57)

So

> rather than spending each session seeking to uncover
> traumatic events of the past, I would attempt to under-
> stand which traumatic elements are being brought to
> my attention by the analytic GPS signal provided by
> the patient and other characters in the session.
>
> (Ferro 2016b, pp. 55–56)

This monitoring, in another metaphor, 'allows the analyst
in his asymmetric position of "chef" to keep on tasting the
food and to continually make adjustments while cooking,
adding either salt or sugar as well as introducing new in-
gredients' (Ferro [2007] 2011, pp. 128–129).

For example,

> Paolo … tells me about his attempts to fix his Vespa,
> which has been lying about forgotten for years. After
> a number of sessions devoted to this subject, I venture
> to suggest that 'sometimes a *vespa* [wasp] will sting.'
> A prolonged silence ensues. In the next session Paolo,
> who has hitherto always come along with a laptop, tells
> me: 'My computer has been struck by lightning and
> it is literally completely burnt out.' So I mitigate the
> pressure of my interpretations, which was intended to
> demechanize certain aspects of the patient, but when
> I later return to a more pungent interpretative regime,
> there appears 'the neighbour who collects weapons and
> who seemed to be aiming a threatening submachine
> gun.' When I return to a more playful style of interpre-
> tation, Paolo mentions the neighbour again, saying that
> his gun—now he has had a clear view of it!—has a red

plug on top of it. It is manifestly a toy weapon, so there is no reason to be worried.

(Ferro and Civitarese 2015, pp. 16–17)

A patient might report: 'Today I had to run away from a dog that wanted to bite me'. Or 'Today my cousin absolutely hit the mark with the medicine he gave me'. Or 'I went to my grandmother's for supper, but she only gave me some thin soup, so I ended up starving hungry and furious'.

> [T]he patient—or any other element of the field—is constantly signalling the patient's perception of the analyst's intervention (or silence), and this becomes the starting point for subsequent adjustments made with a view to keeping a process of transformation active and ensuring that it is not blocked by an excess of persecution or by insufficient interpretive activity. Even infancy and sexuality can become entities that are not only significant in and of themselves, but also characters signalling how the field is functioning.
>
> (Ferro 2009, p. 213)

Sexuality

Sexuality in the session, narrated or in the form of a 'countertransference' experience, indeed needs to be understood as a mode of communication, an indicator of the quality of emotional contact in the current field and a live commentary on it. 'When ♀ and ♂ [container and contained] first relate to each other, this is in effect the first sexual relationship between the mind and another mind, and between a mind and itself' (Ferro [2006] 2009, pp. 134–135). Sexuality is a 'choice of narrative genre and is to the α-element as the plot is to the fabula' (Ferro [1999] 2006, p. 47), a character, or linkage between characters.

It can, of course, be thought of in many other ways, in terms of infantile sexuality or real external sexuality (Freud), or of a sexuality of internal objects and their relations (Klein). Or it might be seen as

> a narration in and of the field *in* one *of* the many 'possible dialects' of the narrative derivatives of the α-elements – that is, a literary genre, which is no more, but no less, meaningful than any other genre … sexuality in a session is the mating of minds – the 'quality' and 'modality' of the meeting of the β-element with the α-function, the handling of thoughts and their communication through the Ps <-> D oscillation, the ♀♂ interaction, and *the way in which all this is narrated.*
>
> (Ferro [1999] 2006, p. 40. See too Ferro 2000a)

In the field-based approach, 'we are constantly having sex and nothing but sex', in that analyst and patient are relating to each other, and

> this relationship *is sex*, even if it follows from the necessary rules of abstinence that we have chaste sex. However, it is certainly not chaste with regard to the emotions activated and experienced, and to the fantasising, also in sexual terms, of the continuous matings *between minds* – the sexuality of the vicissitudes of ♀ to ♂ and β to α.
>
> (Ferro [1999] 2006, p. 48)

Indeed the analytic session necessarily *activates* the sensory/somatic realm of beta-elements. As the analyst Peter Goldberg has put it, 'engagement at the psychosensory level has a distinctive erotics of its own, constituted not in the desire for the object, but in the intense need and pleasure to join with, to enter the domain of shared states' larger than oneself (Goldberg 2023). In this view, analysis depends less on the frustration of sexual desire than on a 'syncretic erotics of embodied at-onement' which can connect us to the 'collective sensorial experience' that we need to help us become persons. In this trans-individual domain – an analysis, a functioning field, music, speech, laughter, or catching a ball – 'the sensory motor hums along' (Goldberg 2022), and wild and untamed thoughts might find embodiment.[4]

Ferro summarises

Ferro has outlined some of the alternating actions he finds himself carrying out when he listens to a patient.

I participate fully in the manifest content of what he is saying. I let myself be permeated, I yield to the fascination of his story, often making minimal, enzymatic interventions which, apart from letting him know 'I get what you say' or 'I'm in synch', contribute to the development of the story itself. I participate with restraint but without being over-fearful of polluting, since I know that, whatever happens, the grey threads of my possible neutrality would enter the field in the very same way as the red threads of my emotional involvement.

Periodically I take all the *role of the geographer*, someone who takes bearings, as it were: now what do you want to communicate through what you are saying … ? The two levels of listening create interconnections. Generally, I resist the temptation to be a map maker.

Above all I tried to grasp the emotions present … the emotional colouring of what he says, which often I tend to emphasize. I also give great importance to the patient's response to what I say, and this helps me modulate my subsequent comments.

But I also know that while this constantly changing analytic dialogue is going on … opening and closing worlds, what is at stake is also another deeper dialogue between the patient's continuous projective identifications and my ability/inability to engage in reverie. I absorb sensoriality, musicality, tone, protoemotional states:[5] this often turns into images, consistent or seemingly inconsistent with other listening vertices.

There is yet another type of listening that shifts the focus from receiving content to the quality of the patient's mental functioning. I know that what he tells me on the manifest level is a way of bodying forth his dream thought; this is actually what interests me – as is the manifestation of what this produces.

For me manifest content has at most the same value as any other content: a childhood memory, an episode from everyday life, a sex scene, a film seen on television – for me as an analyst at work they all have exactly the same communicative value.

Progressively the session becomes a dream, or perhaps it would be better to say a film, which I observe and in which I participate. However, I always (or almost always) know that I am interested in improving the quality of the patient's apparatus for dreaming and hence for thinking.

(Ferro [2007] 2011, pp. 164–165)

Pluriverse

Psychoanalysis, said Bion, is a probe that expands the field of its investigation 'so that, the further we penetrate into the unconscious, the more work awaits us – unless we strive for a situation in which "the revolutionary becomes respectable – a barrier against revolution"' (Ferro [2002] 2013, p. 61, citing Bion 1979, p. 256).

The 'constantly expanding oneiric holographic field' (Ferro 2009, p. 209), inherently dynamic and unstable, 'has no limits apart from those of its perennial expansiveness. Listening in the analytic field is 360-degree listening' (Ferro 2017b, p. 73), for the field is capable of generating 'an infinity of affective storylines' (Ferro [2014] 2019, p. 35). Or, as Ferro quotes Corrao, it is 'a system with an infinite number of degrees of freedom, and these degrees have an infinite number of possible values which the system takes on at every point in space and every moment in time' (Corrao, unreferenced, Ferro [1992] 1999, pp. 17–18).

As new possibilities for play, dreaming, metaphor, and reverie are gradually introduced, and new characters, dramas, and subplots appear, in ever-evolving interrelation, it is 'tantamount to adding new dimensions or worlds to the field'. The field is thus, 'as a rule, multidimensional—it is a *pluriverse*' (Civitarese and Ferro 2013, p. 196). A 'valid comparison might be with the universe as it is understood today' (Ferro and Basile [2009] 2018, p. 5).

Ferro has also conceptualised it as 'a vast lake ... in which there is time for characters to emerge, to sink into the depths, to return to the background or to take the stage again' (Ferro and Basile [2009] 2018, p. 2). It creates the ecological conditions in which the embryonic or the hitherto unobservable might start to find specific form.

The field has a temporal as well as a spatial dimension, a vertical as well as a horizontal plane, for both the patient's and the analyst's transgenerational histories enter it, including the history of the analyst's relationship to psychoanalytic knowledge itself. The journey through these different planes and vectors might be said to be what constitutes the field. Analysis could thus be pictured 'as an amazing machine that allows us to travel in space and time, a space and a time that are beyond doubt equally present at the very heart of the session' (Ferro and Pizzuti 2001, paras 60 and 61, and see Ferro 2000c, p. 20). Time

> enters the session in the form of very diverse temporalities. There is the infinity of possible worlds that will be born from the encounter between analyst and patient from future narratives, from the present of the communication, from the personal past of the patient.
>
> (Ferro and Pizzuti 2001, para 108)

The field is also impossible to grasp in the actual moments of its generation and transformation.

> Bion suggests that only the present can be a conscious datum. The field may be known from the narrative that

takes shape in the session, but this is already out of date at the very moment it is accomplished. In fact, new characters, new emotional forces are continually waiting to be given form, waiting for authors. The gestalt that takes shape is absolutely new, but it can only be described or apprehended afterwards, in the *après-coup*.

(Ferro and Pizzuti 2001, paras 109–110)

In it, micro-transformations occur

without passing by way of active interpretations on the analyst's part. This recalls the conception of Abadi … who named the analytic situation as a self-interpreting context, in the sense that it is the field itself that evolves, that makes its way.

(Ferro and Pizzuti 2001, para 92)

'I look closely at what we "produce" together and what we "cook" together. At some point I have the feeling that the session lives its own life and that the field performs on its own' (Ferro [2007] 2011, p. 165). In this sense, the field does its own work as an ever-expanding container.

Selected fact

But this cannot be the whole picture. If 'our field is to be navigators without a compass and creators, together with the patient, of the unconscious' (Ferro and Nicoli [2017] 2018, pp. 5–6), at some point, for transformation to be consolidated, an ordering principle needs to emerge, what Bion called a 'selected fact'. Putting it another way, the outlines of a 'fabula' need to emerge, which may inform the continuing elaboration of the story.

'The selected fact', Bion wrote, 'is the name of an emotional experience, the emotional experience of a sense of discovery of coherence; its significance is ... epistemological and the relationship of selected facts must not be assumed to be logical' (Bion [1962] 1991, p. 73). Bion adopted the idea from the mathematician Henri Poincaré: the selected fact is 'that by which coherence and meaning is given to facts already known but whose relatedness has not hitherto been seen' (Bion [1963] 2018, p. 19).

The field, like a work of fiction, throws up a plethora of pictograms and characters. But analytic work has to develop 'from a purely chromatic depiction of sensations to a figurative technique, which entails the recognition and description of [the patient's] own feelings and emotions' (Ferro [1992] 1997, p. 48), and the forms, which cannot be assumed to be logical, of their connectedness.

In a famous passage in *Bleak House*, Dickens posed the question:

> What connexion can there be between the place in Lincolnshire, the house in town, the Mercury in powder, and the whereabout of Jo the outlaw with the broom, who had that distant ray of light upon him when he swept the churchyard-step? What connexion can there have been between many people in the innumerable histories of this world, who, from opposite sides of great gulfs, have, nevertheless, been very curiously brought together!
>
> (Dickens [1853] 2011, p. 256)

For the analyst, like the novelist whose work is taking shape, 'at one point one of these pictograms, instead of remaining hidden from myself, becomes something with which I get into contact' (Ferro and Nicoli [2017] 2018, p. 75).

The process involves oscillation 'between Negative Capability – maximal doubt, uncertainty and openness to possible meanings', and

> the strong choice of an interpretative hypothesis which arises from an emotion that aggregates what was dispersed ... into a gestalt that closes the possible senses in favour of a prevalent sense, which in turn univocally reorganises from a given vertex what has formed in the field.
>
> (Ferro [1999] 2006, pp. 7–9)

The selected fact is a development of the analyst's, and the field's, dream of the patient.

Sometimes a 'selected fact' might be a thread running through the narration of the immediate relational situation, leading to a sort of intermediate interpretation which indirectly and figuratively names an emotion emerging in the field, or perhaps, as in this example, a mixture of emotions connected to a revolution that may already be underway.

> I tell Lucio that I shall be away for a couple of weeks (for professional reasons) ... He begins the next session by saying that *he has not had any dreams*. He then tells me that he took the cat along to be neutered and that he feels quite calm. He adds that he has met with one of the leaders of a pacifist association, who has been abandoned by his wife and weeps inconsolably ...
>
> I tell him that, if we were to look at these two communications as if they were two dreams ... we might

think that he was worried that, if the cat had not been neutered, it might perhaps scratch me [and] who knows what might happen if the member of the pacifist organisation who cried because of *my* cheating on him, even if the cheating was in a way 'justified'... was actually the Mexican revolutionary Pancho Villa or ... the Italian national hero Garibaldi.

(Ferro and Civitarese 2015, pp. 18–19)

'Like a good surfer, the analyst must pick out the right wave ... and let herself be carried by it until she makes it safely to shore' (Civitarese 2023, p. 19), an experience which might be accompanied by an 'eerie feeling' (Reiner 2023, p. 36).

A supervisee of Ferro's speaks of a patient who has been suffering from sometimes intolerable 'pins and needles in one of his feet'. He says he has had various neurological appointments, electromyograms, and two aborted psychotherapies. Ferro starts feeling anxious; he feels he has nothing to say: 'facts, facts, and nothing but facts'. The colleague meanwhile is telling him that the patient is concrete, factual, and hence terribly boring.

Ferro reports that meanwhile he is thinking: '"foot gone to sleep," walking, not being able to run, kicking, the film *A Man Called Horse*, but nothing comes together in my mind as a genuine reverie. There is only the lubricant working on the gears'.

The patient goes on to speak about his sense of guilt or shame and says that as a child he often felt lonely, abandoned, and excluded. He smothered the emotions that he was not allowed to experience. There were episodes of loss of control and of rage: once, after a few drinks, he had told a friend's father to go to hell. A notion of rage/ loss of control/guilt begins to form in Ferro's mind. The colleague reports that a film-director friend of the patient's has hired him for an advertising spot for Red Bull.

Only at this point does everything come together for me in a condensed image: a bull pawing the ground before charging. And only then does my colleague add that the patient sometimes makes excessive use of Red Bull. Only now does the *selected fact* become organized and alive—not only the Red Bull, but also what bulls do before hurling themselves at the toreador, or before charging … pawing the ground as if suffering from pins and needles and needing to discharge its tension. So here we see the Red Bull, freeze-dried, condensed, and concretized in the symptom. The need now is to permit the Red Bull and all its rage and fury to emerge from the paw/ claustrum in which it had been shut away, so as to gain access to all possible histories culminating in the putting into images, words, and dreams of the fury the patient had always been afraid of not being able to express. The crystallization of this image ultimately provided me with an interpretative organizer of my thought.

(Ferro 2015a, pp. 515–516)

Such is the digestive process which must be gone through in the analyst's internal laboratory, perhaps with the help of another, a supervisor, or a patient, before a 'selected fact' can crystallise into an image. An effective interpretation can only be 'the final act' of this process (Ferro [2007], p. 106). The analyst, insisted Bion, must earn the right to interpret (Reiner 2023, p. 66).

Bastions

Necessarily implicated, the analyst will inevitably experience times when no such fact emerges. If the term 'countertransference' does still have a value, it might be as a pointer to 'a dysfunction in the field signalled by a part of it' (Ferro and Pizzuti 2001, para 8), 'a useful episode of indigestion – [a signal] that the field is permeated with beta-elements, which it has not been possible for the analyst's alpha-function to transform into alpha', causing a 'jamming' (Ferro [1999] 2006, p. 101). The analyst has contracted the field's illness.

When the analyst's listening and alpha-function are blocked, 'the criss-crossing flow of projective identifications between the participants will lead to pockets of "resistance"' – in the couple, Ferro stresses, not the patient. These are the zones that the Barangers christened 'bastions': obstacles to analytic progress that 'tend to paralyse all movement towards mentalization and insight' (Bezoari and Ferro 1989, p. 1034). Replacing the doctrine of 'resistance' with the concept of the co-generated 'bastion' radically reduces the risk of laying the blame on the patient.

A bastion brings 'a feeling that nothing is happening, and that narratives are stereotyped' (Cassorla 2005, p. 702). Initially the Barangers did refer to the bastion as belonging to the patient; only later did they consider it a 'precipitate' of the field, which 'arises, in unconsciousness and in silence, out of a complicity between the two protagonists to protect an attachment which must not be uncovered'. It is itself a new formation of the field, 'around a shared fantasy assembly which implicates important areas of the personal history of both participants and attributes a stereotyped imaginary role to each' (Baranger, Baranger and Mom 1983, p. 2, cited in Cassorla 2005, p. 702).

It is thus

> necessary to be on one's guard … against those col-
> lusions which distort the analytic dialogue, producing
> phenomena of falsification, pseudo-insight, and inter-
> pretative exercises which are formally correct but lack-
> ing in emotional resonance …
>
> (Bezoari and Ferro 1989, pp. 1038–1040)

A bastion functions like a symptom, often taking the form of 'a stopper to prevent the emergence of something unknown both to the patient and to ourselves, but about which we ought sooner or later to become capable of dreaming together'. It might also be thought of as

> negative reverie, (– R), partially or totally blocked
> reverie—perhaps even a situation of reversed function-
> ing, in which the mind that is supposed to receive and
> transform projects things into the mind that wants and
> needs to evacuate and find a space and method to man-
> age proto-emotions.

It is a situation of trauma, 'exposure to more beta-elements than one can receive and transform, either by oneself or with the other's help' (Ferro and Civitarese 2015, p. 20).[6]

Since it is a specific pathology of the analytical field, the analyst and the patient need to work together to modify it, transforming those aspects of the relationship 'previously dominated by confused, manipulatory and narcissistic modalities' into 'an object-relation in which separation and communication are stressed' (Bezoari and Ferro 1989, p. 1034). A 'second glance' is called for. Whatever we call the analyst's or patient's contributions – 'interpretations', 'associations', 'memories', or 'dreams' (or better, 'accounts of dreams') – is not very important. What matters 'is the transformative function actually performed by these elements of the dialogue, in the direction of symbolic expression and *thinkability*' (Bezoari and Ferro 1989, p. 1034).

In fact, such malfunctions of the relationship, its blind spots to itself, are essential to the work. 'As M. and W. Baranger state (1961–62), "it is part of the analyst's function to let himself become involved in these configurations."' (Bezoari and Ferro 1991/1992a, pp. 30–32).

> [T]he patient's illness will infect the field, which will contract the same illness; it must then be cured by returning a new and transformed type of functioning to the patient. And this transformation will take place solely in the here-and-now of the session!
>
> (Ferro 2015a, p. 523)

A child patient, Claudia, with a diagnosis of mental handicap, feels bombarded by hyper-stimulation, related to the anxious demands of her parents, to which Ferro also responds, and which he re-enacts. At their first meeting, he communicates his sense of urgency to her, unwittingly adopting as his own Claudia's apparent 'inability to think and to understand'. He asks her if she'd like to do a drawing. 'She makes some totally incomprehensible scribbles. She doesn't speak to me but goes on drawing in the same way for the whole hour'.

At the second meeting, Ferro tries 'to shelve what I know about Claudia and prepare myself for a meeting with a girl I have never met'. The pair begin to make some meaningful contact until Ferro once again finds himself 'unable to wait, to tolerate uncertainty, to give Claudia time'; she makes another structureless, incomprehensible picture. Only when he asks if she has always felt that others have pressured her and made her do things in a hurry, not giving her time to think, does Claudia show relief and begin to speak.

The patient's problem has become the problem of the couple, to be

> worked through by the analyst before it can be expressed in words, or 'realised' (Bion), as a new kind of relationship with the child. The child, in turn, can then adopt the new way of relating that she has been shown, and experience it directly.
>
> (Ferro [1992] 1999, pp. 71–73)

Ferro notes that the model he was using at that time was more relational than field-oriented, and that now he would have tried not to extract meaning but to construct a story together with Claudia (Ferro [1992] 1999, p. 74). The important thing is that he was able, by means of his 'second look', to attune to her and her problem, and by the surest means, 'in the field', through negotiation of a 'bastion'. A 'third' is often needed to enable a second look. The field model provides an additional resource: the field itself, if the analyst is sufficiently alert to the feedback it offers, works as such a 'third'.

The analyst's responsibility

Co-operation and reciprocity do not mean total symmetry or equality, as should be clear from the vignette above. It is this that essentially distinguishes post-Bionian field theory from the Relational School. The analyst retains a responsibility – not least, for protecting the patient from the analyst's own projective identifications, as well as for maintaining the setting and its physical and temporal boundaries. In generating the field function, 'the preponderant part is played by the analyst and the lesser part by the patient ... There is an asymmetry in their respective functions' (Ferro and Pizzuti 2001, para 93).

At the same time, the analyst – to remind ourselves – is not an invariant in the field but thoroughly, unconsciously implicated. Ferro underlines this 'leitmotif' of Bion's work, 'the *entirely new way in which the analyst's mind, his functioning and his dysfunctions enter the field*. In Bion's view, the analyst is present with all the weight of his mental life' (Ferro [1992] 1999, p. 11]. He must therefore 'find who his patient is and ... to do so must truly find a place within himself' (Ferro [2007] 2011, p. 153). 'What ridiculous, pathetic monsters we appear if we are courageous enough to look at ourselves through the eyes of the patient and through what the patient tells us from his perspective' (Ferro [2007] 2011, p. 167). '[T]hinking is painful and dangerous, and entails a constant process of calling ourselves into question' (Ferro [2002] 2013, p. 61).

Such openness is in itself transformative.

As a therapeutic factor, we propose the quality of the analyst's mental functioning in the session, and in particular his endowment of receptivity, flexibility, and capacity for transformation, tolerance, and patience. When these enter the field, they effect previously unthinkable transformations.

(Ferro and Civitarese 2016, p. 316)

Field theory clearly calls for constant reflexivity on the part of the analyst, as well as the maintenance of his principal working instrument, his mental life (Ferro 2009, p. 219). Bastions, situations of negative reverie, 'are … narrated in an infinite number of scripts' (Ferro and Civitarese 2015, p. 20) – but the analyst must be able to hear and make use of them. The mind of the analyst must be 'sufficiently mobile and capable of self-repair; otherwise one is likely to be heading for an impasse' (Ferro [2007] 2011, p. 170). He/she needs to try to stay in good shape, by attending one kind of mental-emotional gym or another.

The heart of the analyst's function is 'to act as an enzyme that catalyses transformations in the consulting room' (Ferro 2013, p. 106). 'The nature of the contact barrier', as Bion emphasised,

will depend on the nature of the supply of alpha-elements and on the manner of their relationship to each other. They may cohere. They may be agglomerated. They may be ordered sequentially to give the appearance of narrative (at least in the form in which the contact barrier may reveal itself in a dream). They may be ordered logically. They may be ordered geometrically.

(Bion [1962] 1991, p. 17)

What is crucial is the analyst's readiness to extend the combinatory possibilities of alpha-elements, to embrace and expand her own dreaming capacities, and thus to identify a 'selected fact'.

Ferro and Bezoari initially framed the analyst's task in terms of guaranteeing 'a microclimate suited to allowing the transferential phenomena to develop in a relational sense'. They saw the specific potential of the analytic situation as 'the opportunity it offers the patient to structure the relational field with his projective identifications, through which he can call attention to his unsatisfied needs for mental growth and the unresolved conflicts of his affective life' (Bezoari and Ferro 1991, pp. 30 and 32, and 1992a, pp. 59 and 61).

As the emphasis shifted towards the field as co-structured, the analyst's responsibility could be more simply summed up: 'to safeguard the setting; stimulate the couple's dreaming' (Ferro [2013] 2018, p. 115). The setting too, internal and external, has a therapeutic or proto-therapeutic function: 'the analytic situation can act as an incubator ... The analyst's principal task is to safeguard the delicate and decisive transitional area between the spoken and the unspoken, the experienced and the thought, the self and the non-self' (Bezoari and Ferro 1992a, p. 59). Thus it is important to maintain one's internal setting, something 'beyond countertransference', about which Michael Parsons has persuasively written (Parsons 2007).

'Field theory radically changes how we listen to the patient's communication, which will be seen as also a product of the quality of the analyst's mental functioning or malfunctioning' (Ferro 2005, pp. 93–94). 'There is no patient who does not speak to us of our own out-of-the-way and often silent wildernesses' (Ferro [2007] 2011, p. 118).

In the session before one Ferro has had to cancel, Gioacchino talks about his wife 'who is affectionate but avoids
sexual involvement'. Clearly he is referring to the missing
session, having fewer sessions, and the experience of distance and lack of interest on the part of the other. There is
also a transferential echo, in that Gioacchino's mother was
not as concerned and passionate as he would have wanted
her to be. All these levels could have been interpreted, but
Ferro, listening to the words as an 'echography' of the couple's current functioning, does not do this. 'What is not so
easy to detect', Ferro writes, 'is the affective truth about the
mental functioning of the analyst that the patient is express-
ing': 'attentive and interested but with his passions elsewhere, saturated by other situations'.

> Only this kind of listening is in my opinion able to
> give the analyst's receptivity a greater degree of pas-
> sion in the consulting room (even when part of his oc-
> clusion is the result of having internalised the mother
> who occludes passionate valences or the cold side of
> Gioacchino himself). Working on these issues by offer-
> ing premature clarification would be like decorating a
> Sicilian *cassata* with candied fruit and sponge cake be-
> fore preparing the mixture of ricotta sugar and chopped
> chocolate. Only once the mixture is ready does the
> decoration, however essential, make and acquire sense.
> Mixing is the operation that takes place in the consult-
> ing room, in the mind of the analyst in contact with the
> mind of the patient with the transformations that are
> made ... It is up to the wisdom (and perhaps uncon-
> sciousness) of the pastry chef to open his heart to the
> *cassata* and at least to work on the basic mixture.

(Ferro [2007] 2011, p. 167)

Changing vertices

Readiness to take a second look, to have an ear for feedback and 'supervision' from the field, to maintain the kind of questioning vigilance that might alert one to the presence of a bastion, and, in addition, to take courage from one's predecessors and exemplars – all this contributes to the radical reflexiveness, the quality of attention, enshrined in the post-Bionian field approach.

Laura is reluctant to lie on Ferro's couch.

> Laura, entering the consulting room before me and heading for the analysis area, in one bound ensconced herself in my armchair! I was dumbfounded. Various courses of action (₩ ☹ ₡#?⚔ ☂⚔<⚔<‼☞━☜ 😀 ???✈♥!) flashed through my mind. Remarking to her that the couch must apparently be such a terrible experience that she first needed to see if I could stand it, I then calmly made for the couch and lay down on it. Finally, we had a proper analytic situation, even if the roles were seemingly reversed. I was greatly helped in all of this by my experience as a child analyst, which had over time accustomed me to stop holding the setting in veneration, and I enacted what I would later have called a *transformation into play*. To be honest, I was also helped by recalling—perhaps not accurately—that when Marie Bonaparte was suffering later in life from rheumatism, she too would lie down on the couch.
>
> (Ferro and Civitarese 2016, p. 313)

The ability to change vertices, literally in this case, makes room for a more generous, appreciative stance. Communications can be 'dreamed' in different ways, for 'partially alphabetised aspects (real conglomerates of balpha elements) ... take on various guises ... which need to be monitored'. If the analyst is willing to 'reverse the listening perspective', he may, for example, hear a patient who is in conflict with her boss, and does a lot of washing every Sunday, as not merely engaged in obsessive activity connected to a phobia of dirt and to her real-life conflict. She may also be telling a story 'of the work and effort you have to do with your washing machine (alpha-function), washing away the excess of emotions involved in emotional relations' (Ferro [2010] 2015, p. 144).

Oscillations

Perhaps even more important for the conduct of the analytic game is to allow oneself to be caught by and oscillate between different vertices: between, fundamentally, paranoid-schizoid and depressive functioning, as signalled by Bion's double-headed arrow, PS ↔ D. 'Continually falling ill (... the formation of bastions) and continually getting better (the dissolution of the bastions) correspond to the breathing pattern of the field as it expands and collapses all the time' (Ferro [2007] 2011, p. 106). The reflexivenesss required for this is truly Kantian (Bion's thought was firmly grounded in Kant). It is the courage to use one's understanding – 'Sapere aude!', 'Dare to know!' – in the absence of another's guidance (Kant [1784] 1970, pp. 54–60), and to bear one's own emotional, somatic and context-responsive oscillations. 'Do I make use of more classical interventions?' Ferro asks himself. 'I think I do, but only when I am tired or in a bad mood' (Ferro 2015a, p. 524).

The analyst oscillates between 'maximum asymmetry (he has responsibility) and ... maximum symmetry (the functioning of the field is co-determined by analyst and patient)' (Ferro [2014] 2019, p. 11). He/she seeks to maintain 'an oscillatory equilibrium between meanings and affects' (Bezoari and Ferro 1992b, p. 394) or, to look at this from a slightly different vertex,

> to keep two aspects in balance—namely, the usefulness for the actors in, and authors of, the analytic dialogue of losing themselves in the fiction established by the setting (which means intimacy, closeness, spontaneity, emotional intensity, and authenticity), and the need to re-emerge from it to gain access to the plurality of the possible worlds in which they are simultaneously living.
>
> (Civitarese and Ferro 2009, p. 196)

In practice, this means moving between 'unsaturated' and 'saturated': a moment comes at which one or other of these 'possible worlds' needs naming, including sometimes the transference situation. Much as Ferro has, increasingly, come to value the transformative potentials of dream and narration, this does not mean, in the way that he and post-Bionian Field Theory are sometimes caricatured, total, self-indulgent abandonment to a world of playful dreaming, 'in which patient and analyst do nothing but exchange vague and ethereal fantasies' (Civitarese 2023, p. 97) – a Peter Pan version of psychoanalysis. For 'if the "transformational" space that makes use of a conversational style is one of the driving forces of ... analysis, it is also true that sometimes direct interpretation is what opens up new horizons' (Ferro [2007] 2011, p. 23), and it is this opening up of new horizons that is the priority.

Ferro has been even more explicit.

> There is no situation where only unsaturated interpretations are appropriate. There is a constant oscillation between the negative capability of the analyst, their being able to remain in the PS position without feeling persecuted, and the need for a selected fact, provided that the selected fact really arises from an emotion that the analyst feels there and then. I thought about what Bion says about interpretation; that it must cover the field of sense, myth and passion (Bion 1963, p. 11). This means that it is necessary to interpret something the patient can touch and see, something that must be there. If there is no 'sensual' factor, there is no point in interpreting.
>
> (Ferro 2013, pp. 110–111)

Certainly, 'interpretation, before becoming a classical transference interpretation, must often go on a long journey' moving, Ferro has schematically suggested, 'from an unsaturated interpretation in the field to an unsaturated interpretation of the field, right up to an unsaturated interpretation in the transference and a saturated transference interpretation' (Ferro [2010] 2015, p. 139). And a patient who dreams of being tied to a post ready to be shot, but the firing squad never fires, may be responding to the analyst's over-insistence on unsaturated interpretation (Ferro 2013, pp. 110–111).

There is also a tension between different listening vertices and levels as informed by the analyst's exposure to different analytic schools. Being able to bear and internalise this particular tension might allow a freer internal oscillation between vertices. By keeping in mind different theoretical scenarios, the analyst will 'open himself up for further narrative operations' (Ferro [2007] 2011, p. 75). Such oscillation is, in Ferro's view, vital for the development of the tools of analytic thinking outside the consulting room. We need to be able to use 'that electricity, that potential difference that arises from a series of oscillations between different points of view' (Ferro [2014] 2019 p. 70).

Oscillation is a property of analyst, patient and field together. Ferro's 'dream' of a patient, Pierandrea, is that he alternates between a 'dehydrated' mode of functioning and uncontainable emotional exuberance. He experiences the analyst's interventions either as overwhelming, 'polluting and burning' or, if they are made too much in 'O', that is, too well attuned, as irritating, 'itching', and unsatisfying.

> The oscillation of the patient has … become the oscillation of the analyst's and the field's mode of interpreting. The analyst must distinguish between what he understands (kitchen area) from what he communicates (restaurant area). He should be doing more than simply trying to be in unison: he should be 'acting out' in the session a model of continence that will stand as a third alternative to the twin poles of incontinence and de-affectivised hyper-continence.
>
> (Ferro [2010] 2015, pp. 39–40)

We should not underestimate the sheer, embodied artistry involved in analytic work as Ferro conceives it.

> The art of a psychoanalyst lies precisely in regulating the "breathing" of the analytic field: from the insaturation–inspiration that expands the field to the saturation–expiration that causes the field to collapse in an interpretive choice. In a way, the analyst is positioned as a breathing centre that must constantly modulate—according to necessity—the breaths of the field.
>
> (Ferruta 2003, p. 462)

Psyche-soma

The metaphor of the 'breathing of the field' is not an idle one. For as Bion said, proto-mental distress 'can manifest itself just as well in physical forms as in psychological' (Bion [1961] 1989, p. 102). Mind-body bridge-building is 'certainly problematic', wrote Ferro. But if the analyst and the patient are able 'to keep a firm hold on our capacity for narrative' and stay immersed in the 'dream-pool', good effects can follow; 'if it is eased by the infiltrations of the proto-mental, bodily reality starts to function again' (Ferro [2014] 2019, p. 55).

Metaphor itself, that 'queen of tropes' (Ferro and Civitarese 2015, p. 11), provides a special point of equilibrium between body and mind, since, as we have heard, metaphors are

> pervaded with sensoriality (i.e. they retain the mark of things), while at the same time distancing themselves from things (which they symbolise). They are *sensible ideas* (Carbone, 2008) – that is to say, they combine emotion and thought. They therefore restore a bodily

element to the mind; they reunite psyche and soma; they reforge the 'psychosomatic collusion' (Winnicott 1974, p. 104) that is the foundation of subjectivity; they are dreams that *create* reality and give it a personal meaning.

(Ferro and Civitarese 2015, p. 25)

'Sensible ideas': this is why metaphors might be described as 'the most profound form of thought of which we are capable' (Ferro and Civitarese 2015, p. 94).

If the patient's alpha-function is a 'poem of the mind', and the field is a dream of two minds, the best response, as Baudelaire wrote with regard to paintings, might be another poem (Baudelaire [1846] 1971, p. 143). A poetic response might allow free rein to the sensual qualities of the words themselves, their rhythms, textures, and edges. It might be able to speak directly to the as yet unmetabolised proto-mental and initiate or further a process of beta-to-alpha transformation, from soma to psyche-soma. As Beckett wrote of Joyce,

Nor is he by any means the first to recognize the importance of treating words as something more than mere polite symbols. Shakespeare uses fat, greasy words to express corruption: 'Duller shouldst thou be than the fat weed that rots itself in death on Lethe wharf'. We hear the ooze squelching all through Dickens's description of the Thames in *Great Expectations*. This writing ... is a quintessential extraction of language and painting and gesture, with all the inevitable clarity of the old inarticulation. Here is the savage economy of hieroglyphics. Here words are not the polite contortions of 20th century printer's ink. They are alive. They elbow their way on to the page, and glow and blaze and fade and disappear.

(Beckett 1929, pp. 10–11)

Elaboration, by way of metaphor among other verbal touches pervaded with sensoriality, is how the analyst builds a psycho-somatic bridge to the patient and articulates the field. Like a poet or critic, he/she thus attunes and comes as close as possible to *embodying* the patient's unique, private, unpredictable idiom or thumbprint of alpha-elements and that patient's way of translating and organising them. For 'the style, quality and pictorial genre of the α-element are specific to each human individual; they constitute the mind's most fundamental nucleus of truth in relation to one's emotions and perceptions' (Ferro [1999] 2006, p. 46).

Ogden has beautifully evoked our sensual beginnings as psyche-somas in formation:

the infant's cheek rests against the mother's breast. The contiguity of skin surfaces creates an idiosyncratic shape *that is the infant at that moment.* In other words, the infant's being is, in this way, given sensory definition and a sense of locale.

(Ogden 1991, pp. 382–383)

For Civitarese and Ferro, Ogden puts us in touch with

nothing less than the dawn of meaning, the first transference, the first metaphor … if the child's first 'words' are tactile, they will always retain this sensory, or more properly, somatopsychic quality, even when they are an expression of symbolic thought.

The analyst, taking into account the model of the cheek/ breast interface, respects the patient's

> need for identity. And identity has not only to do with psychic contents but also with the frame around the painting, with the background against which the figure stands out, with the body and its emotions – and does not allow itself to be grasped from a purely logical-rational point of view.
>
> (Civitarese and Ferro 2020, pp. 98–99)

The analyst's task therefore, especially with severe pathologies, is to

> give meaning to the 'white noise' of trauma, to the memories of the body that precede the ego. It is a matter of reconstructing the background from which the reflective consciousness emerges, of re-setting the margins, the frames within which the experience is organized; getting in tune with the music of events, with the inexpressible; restoring sense, which is also making sense for the first time. It is something that we can connect … with the idea of rhythm, to the extent that rhythm is something that is felt and contributes to the creation of meaning, but does not allow itself to be uttered.
>
> (Civitarese and Ferro 2020, pp. 98–99)

'O'

The analytic field opens a way of approaching the unutterable and ineffable, of making 'contact with the depths' (Eigen 2011) – with what Bion, in *Transformations*, named 'O'.

'O' is like 'Kant's thing-in-itself' (Bion 1965, p. 12), and it readily lends itself to mystical interpretation (or dismissal) – for mysticism indeed speaks to those deeply intuitive dimensions of mind for which Bion's writings and the post-Bionian theory of the field make room.

'O' can also be thought about as the 'virtually … psychotic state' from which dream preserves the personality (Bion [1962] 1991, pp. 15–16). It is 'born of the chaos of primitive, psychic thought processes that must be contained in thought without destroying the energy of that primitive mind' (Reiner 2023, pp. 51–52). It is mystery to be approached with respect.

Perhaps, as Grotstein ([2007] 2018) has suggested, we might 'consider these two approaches to O as in a state of necessary oscillation' (Ferro 2015a, p. 514). 'O' is a concept that asserts 'with great force a principle of systematic doubt' (Civitarese 2023, p. 23).

For Ferro 'O', 'the unknowable thing', ultimate truth or reality, is 'the underlying reason why a patient is in analysis', and it is more than can be borne – for 'our species cannot tolerate the harsh, hard impact with reality'. Thus, 'O' requires a 'handle of lies', like a hot frying pan which nevertheless contains 'the excellent fries that truth offers us' (Ferro and Nicoli [2017] 2018, pp. 138–139).

'O' must 'be progressively dreamed … we will never know the real O, we will always know its derivatives, which take the form of a lie. In other words, O has to undergo a *transformation in lie*, which makes it tolerable … any truth, in order to be witnessed, shared, or experienced, needs some room for lies around it' (Ferro and Nicoli [2017] 2018, pp. 138–139). The great storyteller

Oscar Wilde showed his understanding of this in a famous essay, 'The Decay of Lying' (Wilde [1891] 2010). And as Eco wrote, 'If something cannot be used to tell a lie, conversely it cannot be used to tell the truth: it cannot in fact be used "to tell" at all' (Eco 1976, p. 7).

The acquisition of language and entry into the Symbolic incurs loss, the word being a substitute for the ineffable thing itself, or for what was encountered at the moment of the birth of the universe in the chaos of primitive, psychic thought processes. So, wrote Ferro, '"Operation Field Zero Time" is mourning for Reality, that Reality which corresponds to Time Zero, to "O", to the Final (or First) Reality', through which it might be 'alphabetised', transformed into stories and rendered 'into material suitable for the construction of dream' (Ferro 2017b, p. 73). Perhaps it is also a question of yearning, from which we are never free but which must be accompanied by mourning if it is not to overwhelm and immobilise, to ossify into melancholy.

Psyche 'originates from a sacrifice of reality'; alpha-function, dreams, reveries, and narrations are the tools which transform 'O', Truth, into that part of Truth which is bearable for our minds (Ferro 2015a, p. 521). This is why dreams must be seen not as ways 'of making contact with emotional or psychic truth, but … lies capable of bending O to our need for meanings and narrations to organize emotions, affects, circumstances, and further meanings' (Ferro 2015a, p. 520).

A patient is in a state of catastrophic grief, 'where pain is really the O … the central theme that we do not know how to deal with'. Then

the whole analysis will be centred on how to metabolise this boulder of pain, how to transform it into something that can indeed be dreamt, shared, and I would
even say played as a game in a lofty sense. Of course,
we should always consider that for a child a game is a
very serious thing.

(Ferro and Nicoli [2017] 2018, pp. 137–138)

Since contact with 'O' is contact with the proto-mental, it
can bring to life the most primitive, beta-charged aspects
of mind – perhaps the elements Ferro has termed 'beta 2',
'sense impressions of emotional meaning' from the repressed unconscious (Ferro 2015a, p. 514) – and prompt
'catastrophic change', which could be thought about as a
great surge in alphabetisation. Transformations in 'O'

involve a sudden leap in mental growth … achieved by
way of a crisis that may sometimes even include short
periods of depersonalization. Characteristic features of
catastrophic change are violence and subversion of the
system … as well as, for the analyst, awareness of the
emotions of being unable to spare himself or his patients the experience of catastrophic truth. Transformations in O differ from other transformations in that the
former are related to growth in becoming and the latter
to growth in knowing about growth.

(Ferro 2015a, p. 52)[7]

Ferro has defined such transformations in terms of the
long journey of O in column 2 of the Grid, that of lies
and dreams. 'We need to learn how to dance across column 2 and row 3 of the Grid: myths, dreams, and complex

narrations'. 'As Grotstein puts it, what we can do is to transform our perception, our experience of truth (O), into fiction and confer the status of a myth on it' (Ferro 2015a, pp. 521 and 514).

Art and play

We are called to accept that which cannot be known but to which we are constantly drawn, and to accept and begin to enjoy the necessary fictions and lies that enable us to make some bearable contact with it and are part of living. Over time, through the joint, largely unsaturated 'elaboration' of the interpersonal field, we can experience its breathing, its rhythm.

Leopardi would have had no difficulty with this: his poetics of the vague and the indefinite was

> born from this continuous oscillation, or vibration, in which the gaze of the poet (and of the reader as well) is unable to focus on or to encompass completely the object; yet the object, for this very reason, emanates a hidden and mysterious light.

And for him, poetry was 'conceivable only as voice, song, the material emission of sound and breath' (D'Intino 2015, p. lxi).

The rhythmic breathing of the field is felt and contributes to the creation of meaning, but does not allow itself to be uttered. 'That is why the aesthetic experience and the feeling of truth that we associate with it ultimately become a model for analytic work … We get … in tune with the music of events' (Civitarese and Ferro 2020, p. 99).

Thus, Ferro could write: 'The purpose of analysis is to develop the poet, painter or musician who, often unbeknownst to the patient himself, lurks silently within him' (Ferro [2007] 2011, p. 50).

> [W]e are artists, Bion suggests, or, at least we should have the courage to use our skills as artists – after all, don't we all dream at night and during the day? Don't we all compose the poetry of the mind that Freud ([1891] 1953) talks about in his book *On Aphasia*? Don't we all constantly transform sensory reality into images, sounds, colours, all possible kinds of pictograms, audiograms etc. olfactograms, and then assemble these fragments into narratives, paintings, olfactory melodies musical odours, and so on.
> (Ferro and Civitarese 2015, pp. 30–31)

'To shift from a vertex of one "sense" or "system" to another affords a way out of a difficulty that use of one vertex alone makes impossible', wrote Bion in *Transformations* (Bion [1965] 1984, p. 90). He was talking about moving beyond the visual and playing across the senses; he was also alluding to the enrichment and expansion of our emotional repertoires that art and psychoanalysis can bring about and the corresponding loosening of the constraints of a dominant or exclusive way of being.

'Bion [2008], as I was recalling a little while ago, wrote that we should always give the patient a good reason for coming back: a good reason would be that very playing together which eases pain' (Ferro 2017b, pp. 73 and 75).

For Johan Huizinga, in his classic book *Homo Ludens* (1938), play is foundational. It is not symbolic of something else but generative of and in itself, and it is almost by definition aesthetic. Huizinga draws a parallel with poetry.

> The rhythmical or symmetrical arrangement of language, the hitting of the mark by rhyme or assonance, the deliberate disguising of the sense, the artificial and artful construction of phrases – all might be so many utterances of the play spirit.
>
> (Huizinga 1938, p. 132)

Ferro tells a remarkable story about a 'transformation in play'. A child analyst is working with a boy of about seven who starts making paper airplanes and throwing them at her. One of them hits her painfully in the corner of the eye. Normally very composed, the analyst gets angry and finds herself throwing her own paper airplanes back at the child. When one almost hits him in the eye, she is mortified, and stops. She regains her composure, but by then the boy has started cursing and swearing at her.

> To her bemusement, she found herself turning all of these swear words into light-hearted rhyming verses. The boy would swear at her and she would transform his words into rhymes. Little by little the child's anger seemed to wane and he asked if she would have a go at swearing too. Perhaps still flushed by her previous anger and much to the boy's delight, she found this quite easy to do and let out a string of four-letter words. The boy then started turning these words into rhymes of his own.

The airplane game becomes a rhyme game, something enjoyable for both parties. At the end of the session, the boy says he can hardly wait to come again. Over the following sessions, they continue the game. The analyst makes up increasingly interpretive rhymes such as 'The little son of a … was angry because …'. Something very aggressive is transformed into play (Ferro 2018b, pp. 49–50).

The most radical and challenging art must sometimes be enlisted to give an idea of the degree of receptivity and the ability to survive one's own mortification that is needed for a co-created destination to emerge and be experienced. Otherwise, it is

> as if a canvas could give information about how it should be painted: what would become of paintings by Fontana and others in which the canvas is torn all the way to the frame, or those paintings in which the frame itself 'explodes'?
>
> (Ferro [2014] 2019, pp. 3 and 5)[8]

For Ferro and his colleagues, the traditional relationship between art and psychoanalysis needs rethinking. 'Psychoanalysis should not be used, as it so often is, to decipher an artistic text, but … instead art should serve to interpret psychoanalysis … [in] a meeting, a collaboration or an opening' (Ferro and Civitarese 2015, p. 63). They have a parallel function; and the former can illuminate the latter. The opening which art offers would seem to lead to the oscillating poles of pleasure – the pleasure of narrating and representing – and of tragedy, about which Ferro has this to say:

> The paradox of the human species is that tragedy is better for our mind than silent unrepresentability. It is no accident that theatre, cinema and literature, but

also sport, narrate and re-narrate encysted narremes of our species that still belong to the non-experienced mind and not to structural biology. The achievement of analysis … lies in turning back into tragedy what was evacuated in the symptom – itself nevertheless a momento of a hope for thinkability.

(Ferro [2007] 2011, p. 159)

Notes

1 See too with reference to 'characters', Ferro ([1992] 1999, pp. 114–115).
2 There are echoes here of Milner's 'listening with the body' (e.g. Milner 1960) and Winnicott's 'transitional states' between psyche and soma (Winnicott [1971] 1985).
3 'It is not the moment of my clever interpretation that is significant', wrote Winnicott. 'Interpretation outside the ripeness of the material is indoctrination and produces compliance … resistance arises out of interpretation given outside the area of overlap of the patient's and the analyst's playing together' (Winnicott [1971] 1985, pp. 59–60).
4 I am grateful to Richard Morgan-Jones for suggesting this connection with Goldberg's work.
5 There are echoes here with British Independent analysts such as Christopher Bollas and Michael Parsons.
6 The most terrible consequences have, for Ferro, been narrated in Thomas Harris's Hannibal Lecter trilogy (1981, 1988, 1999), which shows uncontainable suffering being violently evacuated upon another (Ferro 2002, p. 19) Lecter embodies Bion's 'H', hate (Bion [1962] 1991, etc.).
7 Perhaps Bion and Rickman's Northfield experiment was a paradigmatic transformation in 'O'. The military and medical system could not restore the shellshocked and demoralised soldiers in the hospital: they were encouraged to choose how and whether to engage with each other, which

led to play, narration, and emotional meaning from which the too-muchness of trauma had shut them away.

8 Lucio Fontana (1899–1968), an artist whose work Ferro is fond of evoking, was born in Argentina to Italian immigrant parents and worked in Milan for much of his life.

Chapter 4

Discussion

Orthodoxy and applied analysis

In Ferro's *Reveries*, there is a story, or prose poem, called 'The Library'. Every night the books plucked up the courage to slip down from their shelves and 'gave voice to the characters they narrated until these last, through continual repetition of their stories, began to take form and unpredictable encounters were possible'. But it was not possible to know these various stories, of love, loss, and betrayal, because each night

> the characters had to return to the books as they had left them and everyone continued to believe in the stories told in the book, which no longer corresponded to what happened at night, in a reality prevented from emerging by a respect for order.
>
> (Ferro [2008] 2015, p. 66)

For Ferro, many macro-social phenomena have the function of 'stopping' unwelcome emotional states; there exists a whole array of 'collective defences against anything that disturbs the "minimal emotional regime" … racism, dogmatism, the delusion of faith-based constructions,

DOI: 10.4324/9781003313311-5

wars, and general stupidity'. For the Epicurean Ferro, religion

> really is the opium of the people – but in the medical sense that opium is an antidote to intolerable pain, the realization namely that the meaning of life is just living it and nothing more, and that there is nothing in life that transcends it.
>
> (Ferro [2007] 2011, pp. 3–4)

It may come as surprise, in this context, that Ferro has been reluctant to join in field-based speculation about the social, cultural, political world outside the consulting room, although the implications of analytic field think-ing for the study of larger groups and culture – the field concept after all originated in the social sciences as well as in physics – are rich and various. They have been de-veloped by figures such as Neri (2009), with his interest in the intersection and overlap of cultural and social fields with the interpersonal and group field, and Morgan-Jones (2010), whose work in organisational consultancy draws on Bion's ([1961] 1989) notion of proto-mentality and how it shapes wider social systems and interactive fields.

When Ferro was asked in 2001 if he thought 'extramural' analytic work was important, particularly institutional work in which the analyst might be immersed in a non-analytic culture, he found himself thinking two contradictory things. On the one hand, extramural analytic work can be

> rich and constructive … a person who, through analy-sis, has been able to pass through and accept profound transformations can certainly be useful in a whole series

of working contexts. On the other hand … for there to
be an analysis, there need to be an analyst, a patient,
and a setting … an analyst without an analysand and a
frame is just a person again like everyone else.

(Ferro and Pizzuti 2001, paras 32–37)

Recently, he has been more outspoken:

we are often ridiculous when we attempt applied psychoanalysis. I think the thing that we are not ridiculous
at is being psychoanalysts: just us, our patient, and our
setting. Then we become something truly important:
people who are able to cope with mental suffering, to
take care of it, to heal it, and metabolise it … this is our
field, this is our speciality.

(Ferro and Nicoli [2017] 2018, p. 5)

Ferro is as Freudian as Freud himself in seeking to protect
psychoanalysis's unique and specific freedom, its capacity to welcome and metabolise intolerable emotional pain
and overwhelming proto-mental energies. In other respects, however, Freud is history for him. Ferro is highly
critical of psychoanalytic orthodoxy and its 'High Priests
of the Known', with their 'sacred fury' (Ferro [2002]
2013, p. 11; 2021, p. 139). Orthodoxy, he has said, is 'a
real danger' (Ferro 2023).

'We cannot … dispense with the level of listening and
interpretation which we predominantly espouse — the oe-
dipal level, the pre-oedipal level, the level of psychotic
anxieties', he wrote in 2009 (Ferro 2009, p. 212).

But as far as its clinical use today is concerned, [Freud's
work] is useless … Things are different if you read

Freud to see the method he used, he dared to change all the time ... I would not find any reason why we should read Freud's work, except for the flavour, the pleasure of knowing history at the time of our grandparents, or to read a few clinical cases that are delightful, but certainly not to do the same to our patients ... in analysis a lot more things happen than those that we know about. Analytic research is naming these things. This is our future, finding out why it works, but we'll find out more the more we will be able to give up grandma's feather hat.

(Ferro and Nicoli [2017] 2018, pp. 47–49)

It is hardly surprising that Ferro's work has attracted criticisms from various psychoanalytic viewpoints, to some of which we shall now turn.

Criticisms

Otto Kernberg has been prominent in noting the degree of Ferro's departure from Freud. This, in his view, has led to a neglect of 'drive and affect theory; early object relations ... attachment, eroticism', the role of 'aggression in determining early normal and pathological structures ... [and] the interactional aspects of unconscious determinants and actual life' (Kernberg 2011, pp. 660–661). Wendy Katz, writing like Kernberg from a broadly ego-psychology perspective, has similarly felt that a focus on 'the narrativizing function' means that 'other layers of experience can easily be missed' (Katz 2013, p. 474).

For Kernberg, 'privileging ... the "field" material and interpreting it in the form of metaphorical narratives may contribute to an unrealistic, fantastic atmosphere in the sessions' (Kernberg 2011, p. 653), risking a dilution of 'the sharpness of the analysis of external reality proper, the patient's responses to it, and the characterologically based defensive operations of the patient's behavior in the session as well as in external reality' (Kernberg 2011, p. 652). Karen Roos (2020) has similarly written of 'Ferro's idealization of dreaming', which can 'give his work an experience-distant quality ... what about the analyst's willingness to suffer drought, not being able to dream?' Might Ferro's 'faith in dreaming' be at the expense of a fuller engagement with the patient at his/her most depleted and lead to a 'pseudo-treatment'? (Roos 2020, p. 852) Might it also lead to 'an impression of Ferro magically translating or decoding characters'? (Roos 2020, p. 851)

Since for Ferro 'everything in the field is co-constructed, transference and countertransference are binary and moot'. This, in Roos's understanding, is to discard a view of countertransference 'as the analyst's emotional-bodily register, his porosity to psychic and somatic reverie ... The analyst's countertransference can mark the trail to unrepresented emotional experience' (Roos 2020, pp. 851–852). 'Ferro's assumption that the patient's stories are the narrative derivative of unconscious waking dreaming runs the risk of overvaluing the significance of language and the function of words as emotional containers' and of neglecting 'the background noises of a patient's nonverbal communication, in the physical movements of his body, hands or face or through the cadence, tone and intensity of his speech' (Roos 2020, p. 852, and see Kernberg 2011, p. 652).

Kernberg's reservations belong within a general critique of the neo-Bionian approach. In particular, 'the concept of beta elements emerging and their transformation into alpha elements during the sessions appears a questionable theoretical framing for the transforming of unconscious elements into conscious ones during the psychoanalytic process'. Bion's concept of proto-emotions, Kernberg claims, can be critiqued in the light of contemporary neurobiology and affect theory: affective experience related to a perceptual environment is stored as affective memory from birth onwards (Panksepp 1998). Kernberg seems to be implying that there is therefore no theoretical need for the process of beta-to-alpha transformation that Bion proposed, even less so with patients able to function verbally (Kernberg 2011, p. 649).

Ferro's colleague Michele Bezoari has also questioned the legitimacy of simply transposing Bion's mother capable of 'dreaming' her baby into life onto the analyst and adult patient. Referring to an earlier co-written paper (Bezoari and Ferro, 1992c), Bezoari notes that two alpha-functions are at work in the consulting room,

> especially with regard to the narrative, evocative and image-creating activities required for (re)producing a dream experience in the analytic dialogue. It would therefore be wrong to apply Bion's model of the internal reverie placed at the disposal of a newborn who lacks it as such to the analytic situation
>
> (Bezoari 2014, pp. 21–22)

Elizabeth Bott Spillius has wondered if interpretative restraint might not be 'as arrogant and condescending as the aggressive display of interpretations intended to show the analyst's omniscience'. And doesn't the container also need 'strong', saturated interpretation to expand? 'Better to err on the side of stretching the container than just fitting in with it' (Bott Spillius 1999, p. xvi–xvii). Katz too points to what may be lost by abandoning traditional, 'saturated' interpretation: the possibility of the patient joining the analyst at a different vertex of observation and having access to thought about himself, thus gaining an experience of participation in what patient and analyst are creating. After all, to follow a Bionian developmental model, the containing mother does sometimes

> engage more directly with the baby's developing ego and sense of self with statements like 'You want me to give you a cookie,' or 'You don't like wearing this hat.' Ferro accepts that a 'saturated' transference interpretation may be necessary at times, but he does not tell us how he identifies these times.
>
> (Katz 2013, pp. 473–474)

For Katz 'the sense of a strong interpersonal chemistry as analyst and patient come together and create a field is somewhat lost' in Ferro's writing. 'In clinical vignettes, the analyst and patient can often seem like shadows who meet in the presence of vivid imaginative forces larger than themselves' (Katz 2013, p. 474, and see Roos 2020, p. 852). Finally, asks Katz, might the 'well-known current of hospitality in the Italian sensibility', a thread in Ferro's work, also be

> tied to the subtle re-emergence … of a certain attitude of authority – the quiet authority of the magnanimous host – that, in valorizing emotional intuition over

self-interrogation, in important ways actually runs counter to the expressed ideology of the analysts who embody it?

(Katz 2013, p. 481)

Sergio Benvenuto, around the turn of the century, detected a 'hermeneutic or "narratological" re-interpretation of analysis' in Italy, whose practitioners 'no longer interpret, they just construct or, rather, deconstruct ... The new keywords are rapport, comprehension, being-with, communication, relationship, intersubjectivity, dialogue ... conversation'. There has, he concluded, been a shift towards the humanistic (Benvenuto 1997, p. 7). He does not specifically name Ferro, but perhaps the criticism is implied.

Responses

A problem with most of these critiques is that they are grounded, like Katz's and Kernberg's, in a two- or even a one-person psychology enshrining a sovereign ego and the notion of a personal unconscious as repository of 'truth'. If they have validity from these points of view, they overlook the potentials offered by the post-Bionian field model for addressing and dissolving some of the problems they also raise.

For example, because 'transference' and 'countertransference' are no longer seen, within this model, as the main axes and motors of analytic work, this does not mean that they do not exist; they have their place within a phenomenological '360-degree' view of the field. But, since the Bionian revolution, they cannot claim their former global explanatory and curative power. It would be strange constantly to defer to them and ignore the insights of Bion and of analytic field theory, just as it would be for a physicist to defer to Newton and overlook particle physics (Ferro [2014] 2019, p. 32).

Bott Spillius's (1992) 'container' seems almost a reified 'thing', independent of the field and its capacities, and of the person and their susceptibilities. The container, she argues, needs robust interpretation to expand it. Ferro would not dispute the principle of expansion, nor the need, at certain junctures, for robust interpretation. Nor would he argue with Katz's (2013) point about the mother who at times engages her baby directly. What is neglected in these critiques is the refinement brought to the analytic process by the idea of emerging 'characters in the field', which let the analyst know that something is ready or pressing for attention. They signal the right moment for 'increasing the emotional voltage that can be tolerated by a mind by way of the development of the instruments for thinking thoughts' (Ferro 2009, p. 212). This is the sense in which the field itself becomes an expanding 'container', requiring only the analyst's (and, the aim is, the patient's) alertness to what is developing in it, signalled by his/her verbal responses. 'Welcome Bill, we've been expecting you!' (Ferro 2016b, p. 56)

Ferro has noted the danger of falling into a sort of Bionian jargon for initiates ('container', 'thought') (Ferro [2007] 2011, p. 56). If the individual's and the field's capacity for dream and play are damaged or out of action, the analyst must, of course, 'suffer drought' (Roos 2020, p. 852). But what Roos, among others, dismisses as an 'idealisation of dreaming' that distances the analyst from the patient's experience is, in Ferro's thinking, nothing more than his attentiveness to the state of the field, which, even in the most severe drought, will not cease to exist as a living potential. In fact depletion or incapacity will already make themselves known as phenomena 'in the field', signalling the need not for its premature elaboration but for its future development and careful nurture. Indeed, as I think Ferro would argue, the shift of attention to the analysis itself, or rather to the field, so that this attention is not directly locked onto the patient in a persecutory way, can help both analyst and patient out of an impasse: in wondering about the state of the field, the analyst becomes freer to engage precisely those dreaming capacities in him- or herself that (in the Bionian model) the patient needs if their own alpha-function is to get re-started or started.

The critique of Ferro's vignettes as lacking in a sense of 'interpersonal chemistry', and of the patient's living three-dimensionality, would also seem to belong to a two-person model, in a humanistic, 'I-Thou' form. Katz's critical but poetic comment, that analyst and patient can come across as 'shadows who meet in the presence of vivid imaginative forces larger than themselves' (Katz 2013, p. 474), is telling: it catches something of the atmosphere of 'working in the field', in which the encounter with thoughts waiting for a thinker, Bion's 'ghosts of the future' (Bion [1965] 1991 p. 95), means contact for both analyst and patient with something larger than themselves, into which both might expand, perhaps with a frisson of awe.

Ferro's vignettes are glimpses of the mental and emotional aliveness that a 'field' awareness can help generate in the analyst. Might we, even so, go along with Katz and Roos and regret the relative absence of the sense of that challenging depth of engagement at which Ferro hints when he writes of patients finding us 'in our own out-of-the-way and often silent wildernesses'? (Ferro [2007] 2011, p. 118) But perhaps this regret is misplaced. Ferro intends his accounts of experiences in the consulting room to be paths 'to provisional ongoing hypotheses, and ... to offer ample margins for discussion and possible dissent' (Ferro [2007] 2011, p. 172), and thus to be relatively 'unsaturated' – just as Bion developed concepts that were as 'empty' as possible, so that the reader might 'live' them in her/his own way. Like Bion, Ferro seems concerned not to forestall or prescribe: the depths to be plumbed are always particular to the couple, and only they can live through the experience.

> When I use vignettes in my texts, they are an attempt to communicate something that is impossible to communicate because it is like trying to convey a recipe: when you write it down it loses its smell, warmth, temperature ... something that only vaguely resembles the dish in its actuality.
>
> (Ferro and Nicoli [2017] 2019, p. 92)

Kernberg and Bezoari, both offering a fundamental critique on the level of theory, question how far it is possible to claim that the adult patient who has reached a certain (unspecified) level of articulacy (i.e., has entered the Symbolic) is still subject to the presence of the proto-mental, of active beta-elements pressing for transformation. It is hard to grasp the substance of this objection, unless, like Kernberg, one is prepared to dismiss Bion's ideas in favour of the findings of neuroscience. But this would still not have to mean discarding them as the metaphors Bion always said they were, nor to ignore their fertility. Bion did not conceive of the process of beta-to-alpha transformation as something completed by a certain point in infancy, but as continuing throughout life. Why, then, should the analyst's alpha-function not remain at the disposal of those aspects of the adult patient as yet unborn and unrepresented?

Perhaps these criticisms underline just how much valuable working resource can be lost if instead of functional metaphor – or hypothesis that opens experiential doors – we rely exclusively on supposed scientific certainties or on elegant theoretical contructs with their own inbuilt invitations to closure. To say this is not to fall back on binary thinking, in which one approach is seen as better than the other. 'Containment', for example, can also usefully be thought about in terms of affect regulation. We are all, in the end, as Ferro so often observes, still mostly working in the dark, in the face of massive unknowns, as neuroscientists would agree.

Some of Ferro's Pavia colleagues have also responded to controversies surrounding the field model. Among these is the question of 'reality'.

'The force of gravity of our naive realism is it so powerful that many analysts continue to misunderstand Freud's lessons and keep to the purely cognitive framework of amateur historicism' (Civitarese and Ferro

2020, p. 33), devoting much energy to constructions and reconstructions, particularly of early experience. Furthermore, writes Civitarese, alongside the rhetoric of countertransference, which can so easily be used as a ready-made defensive prism interposed between the analyst and a closer engagement with the unconscious, there is 'the litany of trauma and testimony', such 'that when faced with real trauma (who decides what falls into this category and what doesn't?) one must suspend analytic listening and only listen in a respectful and receptive manner' – which, he writes, should, of course, always be the case (Civitarese 2023, pp. 96–97).

Mazzacane points to the opposite risk, of a situation 'in which the role of external reality is eclipsed, and anything goes interpretatively', and there is 'a hermeneutic drift in which there is an uncontrolled shift from meaning to meaning, from one connection to another' (Mazzacane 2022, p. 30, and see Mazzacane 2016). This is something that Ferro has noted in Bion's thinking: the risk of a hyper-subjective, quasi-mystical drift in which genuine creativity degenerates into 'an esoterically odd state in which everything is permitted' (Ferro [2007] 2011, p. 56). Such might be the Peter Pan version of psychoanalysis alluded to earlier, in which patient and analyst merely exchange 'vague and ethereal fantasies' (Civitarese 2023, p. 97).

On one level, the problem might be addressed, as we have seen, with the help of narrative theory and the concept of 'the limits of interpretation'. For Mazzacane, the analyst's mind must always be 'open to the way external realities and psychic reality mutually limit each other'. For there will always be conflict between the pressure of external reality to impose itself and the analyst's effort 'to remain in an oneiric structure'. The most important thing is to have this conflict in mind, 'living it in your own skin in the session' (Mazzacane 2022, pp. 29–30).

Mazzacane also takes up a concern with the perils of self-disclosure. Since session material and the tools for thinking are always co-constructed by the analytical couple, there will, he writes, inevitably be a component of self-disclosure on the part of the analyst, intended or not, which must be continuously monitored. The analyst participates in the processes of emotional distance regulation. Whatever is put into play 'must be born from the interaction of the couple' and 'the characteristics of the analysis and the moment on the analytical path'. It 'must always be the subject of reflection … It can put valuable emotional flows into play, without this necessarily implying a reversal of roles in the analytical couple.' 'Self-disclosure', concludes Mazzacane, 'is not a technique, it is simply one of the many ways of being with a patient that is no longer taboo.' (Mazzacane 2022, pp. 29 and 30–32)

But perhaps sometimes we do 'put too much emphasis on the idea of dreaming the session' (Civitarese 2023, pp. 97 and 55). Even analysts profoundly in tune with the dream-field metaphor can feel that it might be too exclusive. Claudio Neri, who as a group as well as individual analyst is a key contributor to post-Bionian and to field thinking, has felt that the idea of the dream-field can be overused, and that it is only one among other active streams and levels of communication (Neri 2016). Howard Levine, perhaps the most astute of Ferro's admirers in the U.S., has also questioned whether the field perspective's 'narrative logical co-constructive implications are always the only optimal response', especially with patients 'deeply enmeshed in pathological organisations' who may not yet have the capacity 'to play the verbal Squiggle Game' and need a 'period of explanation and confrontation'. This is important: often time must be spent, maybe considerable time, building the board before the game can be played.[1]

A field perspective, Levine concludes, must 'remain in oscillating dialogue with other points of view' (Levine (ed.) 2022 p. 35). Or to put it another way, analyst and patient may together need to find out, and continue to find out, about *how* they might be together, without the analyst feeling the need to defer at every turn either to the strictures of established practice or to the technical implications of a field perspective.

Levine also wonders if there is a clear distinction between the saturated and the unsaturated in the processes of at-one-ment and the construction of the container/contained. 'I think [Ferro] believes or gives the impression it is either/or but I think it is more complex and subtle than he may imply. A saturated interpretation is part of the 'O' of the couple at that moment. How could it be otherwise?' (Levine 2021).

And what, asks Morgan-Jones, about patients who suffer from 'untethered agoraphobic anxieties'? Such patientsmay ... discover an impasse within more expansive versions of field theory as they begin to feel increasingly abandoned ... as if the intimacy of close interpretation of primitive and bodily experience is taboo.

(Snell, Morgan-Jones, and Lowenthal 2023, pp. 140–141)

It is hard to imagine Ferro disagreeing with any of this. He has repeatedly insisted on the need for the analyst to be able to 'oscillate' between different theoretical vertices, which, although he feels a field perspective may in important respects look beyond them, does not abolish them (any more than Einstein has written Newton out of the physics books). This perspective can help increase rather than cloud sensitivity to, for example, the agoraphobic patient, whose phobia is likely to appear in the form of one or more 'characters', to be engaged with and elaborated, and why not with direct reference to embodied experience in the room?

Expressions like 'dreaming the session' or 'the shared co-created dream' are

> nothing more than formulas that highlight a style of work in which not only the subjectivity of the patient but also that of the analyst, as well as the unconscious functioning of the couple are taken seriously and as systematically as possible.
>
> (Civitarese, 2023, p. 97)

The centrality of 'transformation in dream' does not mean relentlessly interpreting the unconscious texture of reality; the analyst should *'let herself be rediscovered by it'* (Civitarese 2023, p. 47).

Post-Bionian Field Theory, significantly shaped by Merleau-Ponty's philosophy, is a phenomenological tool. It has the potential to open up body awareness, as is implicit in Ferro's encouragement to analysts to attend to 'sensoriality, musicality, tone, proto-emotional states'

(Ferro [2007] 2011, p. 165). To give less weight to the concept of countertransference is not to overlook 'the analyst's emotional-bodily register, his porosity to psychic and somatic reverie', which can 'mark the trail to unrepresented emotional experience' (Roos 2020, pp. 851–852). Attention to 'the background noises of a patient's non-verbal communication, in the physical movements of his body, hands or face or through the cadence, tone and intensity of his speech' (Roos 2020, p. 852) might indeed help the agoraphobic patient towards a feeling of intimacy.

By dissolving the individualist bias inherent in two-person thinking and opening up a humbling experience of uncertainty as to who thinks or owns what, Ferro's post-Bionian field theory can work to protect, although never, of course, guarantee, against the danger of the analytic 'host' becoming an egoic centre of power (Katz 2013, p. 481) – rather than the responsible guardian of a hospitable environment, the host's proper function. 'There is no definitive remedy', Ferro and Civitarese have said,

> for the possibility that field theory can be used unconsciously as a kind of enactment for the purpose of avoiding pain …. It is true, however, that a radically critical theory, accustomed to systematic doubt and non-authoritarian in spirit, is better equipped … to counteract this risk or to correct its course.
>
> (Ferro and Civitarese 2016, p. 314)

Ferro's challenging model encourages living through an experience with the patient 'in your own skin' (Mazzacane 2022, p. 30). Such embodied experience, as Bion

helps us see, is both individual and social; it emerges out
of the proto-mentality that belongs both to our own individual histories and to our collective humanity, linking us
and giving rise to the cohesion as well as the turbulences
of the group. Field theory puts us in touch with the phenomenological foundations of Bion's thinking and makes
it that much harder, in practice, for us to ignore or sidestep
our mutual implication with one another.

Note

1 'Interpretation when the patient has no capacity to play
  is simply not useful, or causes confusion … *This playing
  has to be spontaneous, and not compliant or acquiescent*,
  if psychotherapy is to be done' (Winnicott [1971] 1985,
  pp 59–60).

Conclusion

'The most felicitous psychoanalytic writings', Ferro and Civitarese have written,

> convey wonder, pleasure, enthusiasm, and a sense of fullness of life extending far beyond the theoretical and practical field in which they originated and to which they belong. They expand the range of sensations to which we are able to respond throughout our lives.
>
> (Ferro and Civitarese 2015, p. 63)

Ferro has maintained an expansive, reasoned, and fundamentally optimistic view of life and therapy, in which, for example, 'the death instinct and destructiveness are not just a curse of the species but a transgenerational accumulation of beta-elements that, in the future, we may be able to metabolise and digest, turning them into creativity and the capacity to experience emotions' (Ferro [2010] 2015, p. 137) – rather, it might be added, than trying to kill them and each other off.

Ferro's practice can in many ways seem as Winnicottian as it is Bionian (and it is certainly distant from the

DOI: 10.4324/9781003313311-6

'Kleinian' Bion of the 1950s and 1960s): the roots in child therapy; the field itself as a kind of Squiggle game; and the emphasis on play and 'aliveness', on interpretative restraint and tact, on reverie, and on respect for the incommunicado and for the patient's need for privacy. There is the adumbration of the field idea in Winnicott's famous 'there is no such thing as an infant' (Winnicott 1960, p. 37 n. 1). But the main theoretical underpinning of Ferro's work is Bionian.

Levine hails Ferro as one of Bion's 'most fertile, productive and creative' descendants, 'the embodiment of Bion's concept [of an analyst]'. He regards Ferro's contributions to contemporary psychoanalysis as 'catalytic, transformational' (Levine 2022, p. 2). Civitarese feels that 'after the invention of the concept of transformation in dream, and moreover remaining faithful to the spirit, if not the letter, of Freud, BFT brings to completion the paradigm shift in psychoanalysis that we have already attributed to Bion' (Civitarese 2023, p. 47).

Ferro himself would not seem quite as ready to embrace the idea of completion. He has adopted a different perspective. On the one hand, as he has repeatedly said, 'there are radical differences in implicit models, in techniques and theories'. On the other, 'No one has shown that one model treats patients better than another; perhaps all we can say with any confidence is that a particular analyst, no matter what his orientation, enjoys our trust' (Ferro [2007] 2011, p. 176).

From psychoanalysis's beginnings, he has said, the analyst-patient couple have been performing 'many more operations than psychoanalysis can conceive of'.

Projective identification already existed in Freud's day and waking dream thought in Klein's. Transformations happen without the analyst being conscious of them. 'So an analyst espousing, say, an old-fashioned drive model, as long as he is able to listen and reflect, will still be receiving β-elements and transforming them into α, while believing he is reconstructing the patient's childhood' (Ferro [2006] 2009, p. 54). Perhaps Levine has put his finger on it. 'We are always stuck with the ontological' (Levine 2023), even when we are being epistemological.

Ferro has said he is 'on a journey towards a pure field model' (Ferro [2014] 2019, p. 79). He does not mean by this some kind of field fundamentalism. The Starship Enterprise's mission is not a colonising one, 'as if there is an unconscious truth and the aim of psychoanalysis is to discover it'. On the contrary, 'finding a meaning is one thing, whereas needing to find it, or having already found it, is another', a sort of disease that 'whether inside or outside the analyst's consulting room … has given rise to dramatic situations such as those always ultimately triggered by fanaticism of any hue' (Ferro 2009, pp. 226–227).

It is a journey that takes us, rather, to 'a horizon of meaning' (Ferro and Civitarese 2015, p. xv) beyond the uncertain frontiers of the known, 'opening up previously unthinkable mental continents – and with them, new questions and doubts, so that we can "emotionally" acquire knowledge of the enormous scale of our ignorance' (Ferro [2002] 2013, pp. 65–66). There is, Ferro says, a macro-oscillation to which all analysts might resonate, born of the 'links between our history with its deep roots and our need for a future: being proud of what we have discovered, being astonished at the new worlds that our instruments continually open up' (Ferro [2014] 2019, p. 70).

The field model is itself only a way of understanding that gives us 'a provisional view of the phenomena we observe. For it to be fertile, each model has to be ephemeral. A model that does not imply its ultimate transience would be supremely anti-knowledge' (Ferro [2007] 2011, p. 50).

[T]he shocking concept that Bion reveals to us … is that there is a process that continually transforms the data we receive from reality … into a movie sequence within our mind …. I think that the waking dream thought is the key to this revolution. But we should not think that history ends with the French Revolution! … I hope with all my heart that within forty years there will be another revolution and that the concept of field will be forgotten.

(Ferro and Nicoli [2017] 2018, p. 60)

References

Ambrosiano, L. and Gaburri, E. (2009) Las Meninas. In A. Ferro and R. Basile (eds.) [2009] 2018.

Barale, R. (ed.) (2006) *Psiche. Dizionario storico di psicologia, psichiatria, psicoanalisi, neuroscienze*. Turin: Einaudi.

Barale, F. and Ferro, A. (1987) Sofferenza mentale nell'analista e sogni di contro-transfert. *Rivista di Psicoanalisi* 33:219–233.

——— (1992) Negative therapeutic reactions and microfractures in analytic communication. In L. Nissum Momigliano and A. Robutti (eds.) 1992.

Baranger, M. (2004) Field theory. In S. Lewkowicz and S. Flechner (eds.) 2005.

Baranger, M. and Baranger, W. (1961–1962) La situación analítica como campo dinámico. *Revista Uruguaya de Psicoanálisis* 4(1):3–54.

——— (1966) Insight in the analytic situation. In R. E. Litman (ed.) 1966.

——— (1990) *La situazione psicoanalitica come campo bipersonale*. Edited by S. Manfredi and A. Ferro. Milan: Cortina.

——— (2008) The analytic situation as a dynamic field. *International Journal of Psychoanalysis* 89:795–826.

——— (2009) *The Work of Confluence. Listening and Interpreting in the Analytic Field*. Edited and Commentary by L. G. Fiorini, London and New York: Routledge.

———— and Mom, J. (1983) Process and non-process in analytic work. *International Journal of Psychoanalysis* 64:1–15.

Baudelaire, C. ([1846] 1971) *Ecrits sur l'Art*, vol. I. Paris: Le Livre de Poche.

Bazzi, D. (2022) Approaches to a contemporary psychoanalytic field theory: From Kurt Lewin, Georges Politzer and José Bleger, to Antonino Ferro and Giuseppe Civitarese. *International Journal of Psychoanalysis* 103(1):46–70.

Beckett, S. ([1929] 1961) Dante … Bruno. Vico, … Joyce. In S. Beckett and others *Our Exagmination Round His Factification for Incamination of 'Work in Progress'*. London: Bradford and Dickens.

Benvenuto, S. (1997) Italy and Psychoanalysis. *European Journal of Psychoanalysis* No. 5. www.journal-psychoanalysis.eu/articles/italy-and-psychoanalysis/ (Consulted 11.01.23).

Bezoari, M. (2014) The dream environment and the analytic environment. *The Italian Psychoanalytic Annual* 8:9–24.

Bezoari, M. and Ferro, A. (1989) Listening, interpretations and transformative functions in the analytical dialogue. *Rivista di Psicoanalisi* 35(4):1012–1050.

———— (1990) Elementos de un modelo del campo analítico: los agregados funcionales. *Revista de Psicoanálisis* 5(6):847–861.

———— (1991) A journey through the bipersonal field of analysis. From roleplaying to transformations in the couple. *Rivista di Psicoanalisisi* 37:4–46.

———— (1992a) From a play between 'parts' to transformations in the couple: Psychoanalysis in a bipersonal field. In L. Nissum Momigliano and A. Robutti (eds.) 1992.

———— (1992b) The oscillation of meanings <-> affects in the analytic couple at work. *Rivista di Psicoanalisi* 38:380–402.

———— ([1992c] 1999). The dream within a field theory: Functional aggregates and narrations. *Journal of Melanie Klein and Object Relations* 17:333–348.

Bion, W. R. ([1961] 1989) *Experiences in Groups and Other Papers*. London and New York: Tavistock/Routledge.

———— ([1962] 1991) *Learning from Experience*. London: Karnac.

———— ([1963] 2018) *Elements of Psychoanalysis*. London: Routledge.

———— ([1965] 1991) *Transformations*. London: Karnac.

———— ([1967] 1980) *Second Thoughts*. London: Karnac.

———— ([1967] 1988) Notes on memory and desire. In E. B. Spillius (ed.) 1988, pp. 17–21.

———— ([1970] 1984) *Attention and Interpretation. A Scientific Approach to Insight in Psycho-Analysis and Groups*. London: Karnac.

———— ([1975, 1977, 1977, 1981] 1991) *A Memoir of the Future*. London and New York: Karnac.

———— ([1977] 1989) *Two Papers: The Grid and Caesura*. London: Karnac.

———— (1978 [2019]) *A Paris Seminar*. In *The Complete Works of W. R. Bion*. Edited by C. Mawson and F. Bion. London: Routledge.

———— (1979) Making the best of a bad job. In W. R. Bion 1987.

———— (1980) *Bion in New York and São Paulo*. Perth: Clunie Press.

———— ([1983] 1985) *Seminari italiani*. Rome: Borla.

———— (1987) *Clinical Seminars and Four Papers*. Edited by F. Bion. Abingdon: Fleetwood Press.

———— (1994) *Cogitations*. New Extended Edition, Edited by F. Bion. London: Karnac.

———— ([2005] 2019) *The Tavistock Seminars*. London and New York: Routledge.

———— (2008) *Clinical Seminars and Other Works*. London: Karnac.

———— and Rickman, J. (1943) Intra-group tensions in therapy - their study as the task of the group. *The Lancet* 242:678–681.

Bion Talamo, P., Merciai, S. A., and Borgogno, F. (2000) *W. R. Bion: Between Past and Future*. London: Karnac.

Bleger, J. ([1967] 1990) *Symbiosis and Ambiguity: The Psychoanalysis of Very Early Development*. London: Free Association Books.

Borgogno, F. and Capello, F. (2011) Psychoanalysis as a 'Journey': A Clinical Method for the Transmission of Psychoanalysis at Universities. *American Imago* 68(1):93–118.

———, Luchetti, A., and Coe. L. M. (eds.) (2016) *Reading Italian Psychoanalysis*. London and New York: Routledge.

Bott Spillius, E. (1999) Introduction to A. Ferro [1992] 1999.

Brenman, E. (1977) The narcissism of the analyst: Its effect in clinical practice. 2nd Conference of European Psycho-Analytical Federation, L'Estoril. In E. Brenman and G. Fornari Spoto (eds.) (2006). *Recovery of the Lost Good Object*. London: Routledge.

Caldwell, L. (2016) A swift glance at Italian psychoanalysis from abroad. In F. Borgogno, A. Luchetti, and L. M. Coe (eds.) 2016.

Calvino, I. ([1979] 1998) *If on a Winter's Night a Traveller*. London: Vintage.

——— ([1988] 1993) *Six Memos for the Next Millennium*. New York: Vintage.

Campbell, D. and Jaffè, R. (2022) *When the Body Speaks. A British-Italian Dialogue*. London and New York: Routledge.

Caparrota, L. and Colazzo Hendriks, M. (2022) The history of the British-Italian Group and acknowledgements. In D. Campbell and R. Jaffè (eds.) 2022.

Carbone, M. (2008) *Proust et les Idées Sensibles*. Paris: Vrin.

Cassorla, R. M. (2005) From Bastion to enactment: The 'non-dream' in the theatre of analysis. *International Journal of Psychoanalysis* 86(3):699–719.

Civitarese, G. ([2010] 2013) *The Violence of Emotions. Bion and post-Bionian Psychoanalysis*. London and New York: Routledge

———— (2014) Bion and the sublime: The origins of an aesthetic paradigm. *International Journal of Psychoanalysis* 95(6):1059–1086.

———— (ed.) (2018) *Bion and Contemporary Psychoanalysis. Reading* A Memoir of the Future. London and New York: Routledge.

———— (2021) Experiences in groups as a key to 'late' Bion. *International Journal of Psychoanalysis* 102:1071–1096.

———— (2023) *Psychoanalytic Field Theory. A Contemporary Introduction*. Routledge Introductions to Contemporary Psychoanalysis. London and New York: Routledge.

———— and Ferro, A. (2013) On the meaning and use of metaphor in analytic field theory. *Psychoanalytic Inquiry* 33:190–209. Reprinted and expanded in A. Ferro and G. Civitarese, 2015.

———— (2020) *A Short Introduction to Psychoanalysis*. London and New York: Routledge.

———— ([2020] 2022) *Playing and Vitality in Psychoanalysis*. London and New York: Routledge.

Conci, M. (2017) Analytic field theory: A dialogical approach, a pluralistic perspective, and the attempt at a new definition. In S. Montana Katz, R. Cassorla, and G. Civitarese (eds.) 2017.

———— (2019) *Freud, Sullivan, Mitchell, Bion, and the Multiple Voices of International Psychoanalysis*. New York: International Psychoanalytic Books.

Corrao F. (1986a) L'interpretazione psicoanalitica come fondazione di un campo ermeneutico e dei suoi funtori. In Società Italiana di Psicoanalisi di Gruppo (eds.) (1987) *L'Interpretazione Psicoanalitica*. Rome: Bulzoni.

———— (1986b) Il concetto di campo come modello teorico. *Gruppo e Funzione Analitica* 7:9–21.

———— (1987) Il narrativo come categoria psicoanalitica. In E. Morpurgo e V. Egidi (eds.) *Psicoanalisi e narrazione*. Ancona: Il Lavoro Editoriale, 1987, and in Corrao, 1998.

———— (1989) Morphology and Transformations of Psycho-analytic Models. In F. Borgogno, A. Luchetti and L. M. Coe (eds.) 2016.

———— (1998) *Orme*. Milan: Cortina.

De Beistegui, M. (2010) Per un'estetica della metafora. In D. Ferrari and P. Godani (eds.) (2009) *La sartoria di Proust. Estetica e costruzione nella 'Recherche'*. Pisa: Edizioni ETS.

De Martis, D. ([1982] 1984) La psicoanalisi come situazione di crisi. In D. De Martis, *Realtà e fantasma nella relazione terapeutica*. Roma: Il Pensiero Scientifico.

Di Chiara, G. (2016) Psychoanalysis in Italy. In F. Borgogno, A. Luchetti, and L. M. Coe (eds.)2016.

Di Chiara, G., Bogani, A., Bravi, G., Robutti, A., Viola, M., and Zanette, M. (1985) Preconcezione edipica e funzione psico-analitica della mente. *Rivista di Psicoanalisi* 31:327–341.

Dickens, C. ([1853] 2011) *Bleak House*. Edited with an Intro-duction and Notes by N. Bradbury. Preface by T. Eagleton. London: Penguin Classics.

Diderot, D. ([1796] 2008) *Jacques the Fatalist*. Oxford: Oxford World's Classics.

Di Donna, L. (2005) Psychoanalysis in Italy: Its origins and evolution. *Fort Da*. 11A(1):35–59.

D'Intino, F. (2015) Introduction to Leopardi. 2015.

Ducrot, O. (1984) *Le dire et le dit*. Paris: Les Editions de Minuit.

Duras M. ([1985] 1987) *La douleur*. London: Fontana.

Eco, U. ([1962 etc.] 1989) *The Open Work*. Translated by A. Concogni. Introduction by D. Robey. Cambridge, MA: Harvard University Press.

———— (1976) *A Theory of Semiotics*. Bloomington and Lon-don: Indiana University Press.

———— ([1979] 1981) *The Role of the Reader*. Bloomington: Indiana University Press.

———— (1990) *The Limits of Interpretation*. Bloomington: Indi-ana University Press.

Eigen, M. (2011) *Contact with the Depths*. London and New York: Routledge

Eizirik, C. L. (2009) Introduction. In W. Baranger and M. Baranger (eds.) 2009.

Fellini, F. (1980) Interview in *Panorama* 18 (14 January 1980).

———— ([2007] 2008) *The Book of Dreams*. Edited by T. Kezich and V. Boarini. New York: Rizzoli International.

Ferrari, A. B. and Garroni, E. (1979) Schema di progetto per uno studio della 'relazione analitica". *Rivista di Psicoanalisi* 25:282–322.

Ferro, A. (1985) Psicoanalisi e favole. *Rivista di Psicoanalisi* 31:216–230.

———— (1987) Il mondo alla rovescia. L'inversione di flusso delle identificazioni proiettive. *Rivista di Psicoanalisi* 33:59–77.

———— ([1992] 1999) *The Bi-Personal Field. Experiences in Child Analysis*. London and New York: Routledge.

———— ([1996] 2013) *In the Analyst's Consulting Room*. London and New York: Routledge.

———— ([1999] 2006) *Psychoanalysis as Therapy and Storytelling*. London and New York: Routledge.

———— (2000a) Sexuality as a narrative genre or dialect in the consulting-room: A radical vertex. In P. Bion Talamo, S. A. Merciai, and F. Borgogno (eds.) 2000.

———— (2000b) Comunicazione personale ai membri del Centro Milanese di Psicoanalisi Cited in F. Borgogno and F. Capello, 2011.

———— (2000c) *La psychanalyse comme oeuvre ouverte*. Preface by F. Guignard. Translated by P. Faugeras. Toulouse: Erès.

———— ([2002] 2013) *Seeds of Illness, Seeds of Recovery. The Genesis of Suffering and the Role of Psychoanalysis*. London and New York: Routledge.

———— (2005) Commentary on M. Baranger [2004], Field Theory, and L. Kanyper [2005] Confrontation between generations as a dynamic field. In S. Lewkowicz and S. Flechner (eds.) 2018.

———— ([2006] 2009) *Mind Works. Technique and Creativity in Psychoanalysis*. London and New York: Routledge.

———— (2006) Clinical implications of Bion's thought. *International Journal of Psychoanalysis* 87:989–1003.

———— ([2007] 2011) *Avoiding Emotions, Living Emotions*. London and New York: Routledge.

———— ([2008] 2015) *Reveries: An Unfettered Mind*. London: Karnac.

———— (2009) Transformations in Dreaming and Characters in the Psychoanalytic Field. *International Journal of Psychoanalysis* 90:209–230.

———— ([2010] 2015) *Torments of the Soul. Psychoanalytic Transformations in Dreaming and Narration*. London and New York: Routledge.

———— (2011) Biographical Note. https://antoninoferro.wordpress.com/2011/10/03/hello-world/ (Consulted 13.03.2022).

———— (2013a) *Supervision in Psychoanalysis. The São Paulo Seminars*. London and New York: Routledge.

———— (2013b) Dream model of the mind. In Ferro (ed.) [2013] 2018.

———— ([2013] 2018) (ed.) *Contemporary Bionian Theory and Technique in Psychoanalysis*. London and New York: Routledge.

———— ([2014] 2019) *Psychoanalysis and Dreams. Bion, the Field and the Viscera of the Mind*. London and New York: Routledge.

———— (2015a) A response that raises many questions. *Psychoanalytic Inquiry* 35(5):512–525.

———— (2015b) *The Field, Virtual Psychoanalytic Museum*. New York: IP Books, Arnold Richards. http://www.virtualpsychoanalyticmuseum.org/gallery-3-time-space/dr-fish-bion-the-field-and-alpha-function/ (Consulted 18.10.2021).

———— (2015c) From Freud to Francis Bacon. *The Italian Psychoanalytic Annual* 9:175–187. At the Origin of Psychic Experience: Becoming Subjects: XVII National Congress of the Italian Psychoanalytic Society (SPI).

———— (ed.) ([2016] 2020) *Psychoanalytic Practice Today: A Post-Bionian Introduction to Psychopathology, Affect and Emotions*. London and New York: Routledge.

———— (2016b) Commentary on Levy and Finnegan. *Journal of the American Psychoanalytic Association* 64:55–62.

———— (2017a) The field evolves. In S. Montana Katz, R. Cassorla, and G. Civitarese (eds.) 2017.

———— (2017b) The Pleasure of the Analytic Hour. XVIII SPI Congress, The Logics of Pleasure, the Ambiguity of Pain Rome, 26–29 May 2015. *The Italian Psychoanalytic Annual* 11:67–78.

———— (2018a) *A Memoir of the Future* and the defence against knowledge. In G. Civitarese (ed.) 2018.

———— (2018b) Bionian and post-Bionian transformations. *Revue Roumaine de Psychanalyse* 11:47–56.

———— (2021) Super-visions. *The Italian Psychoanalytic Annual* 15B(S):137–147.

———— (2022a) Attacks on linking, or uncontainability of beta elements? In G. Civitarese and A. Ferro (eds.) 2022.

———— (2022b) Going for a stroll: The root of emotions. In G. Civitarese and A. Ferro (eds.) 2022.

———— (2023) Characters of the Session, Alpha Dreams and the Negative Grid. Contribution to Third Online Bion Seminar with Antonino Ferro (unpublished). A. Santamaría Psiconálisis México, 05.04.23.

———— and Basile, R. (eds.) ([2009] 2018) *The Analytic Field. A Clinical Concept*. London and New York: Routledge.

———— and Civitarese, G. (2015) *The Analytic Field and Its Transformations*. London: Karnac.

———— (2016) Confrontation in the Bionian model of the analytic field. *Psychoanalytic Inquiry* 36:307–322.

———— (2022) A rhinoceros with a butterfly heart: Antonino Ferro in conversation with Giuseppe Civitarese. *Psychoanalytic Inquiry* 42:378–396.

———— Civitarese, G., Collovà, M., Foresti, G., Mazzacane, F., Molinari, E., and Politi, P. (2012) *Psicoanalisi in giallo. L'analista come detective.* Milano: Raffaello Cortina.

———— and Donna, L. (2005) Conversations with clinicians. Antonino Ferro MD and Luca Donna Ph.D. *Fort Da* 11(1):92–98.

———— Mazzacane, F., and Varrani, E. (2015) *Nel gioco analitico. Lo sviluppo della creatività in psiconalisi da Freud a Queneau.* Milan: Frontiere Della Psiche, Mimesis Edizione.

———— and Melícias, A. B. (2016) Interview with Antonino Ferro by Ana Belchior Melícias. Translation from Italian to English M. do Carmo Sennfelt. *Revista Portuguesa de Psicanálise* 35(2):113–121.

———— and Nicoli, L. ([2017] 2018) *The New Analyst's Guide to the Galaxy. Questions about Contemporary Psychoanalysis.* London and New York: Routledge.

———— and Pizzuti, D. M. (2001) Entretien avec Antonino Ferro. *Cahiers de psychologie clinique* 2001/1(no. 6), pp. 207–223. https://www.cairn.info/revue-cahiers-de-psychologie-clinique-2001-1-page-207.htm (Consulted 16.6.2022).

———— and Stella, G. (2019) *True Lies: Quasi un'apologia della menzogna.* Milan: Mimesis Edizioni.

Ferruta, A. (2003) Review of A. Ferro, *Fattori di malattia, fattori di guarigione* [*Seeds of Illness, Seeds of Health*, 2002]. *International Journal of Psychoanalysis* 84:459–462.

———— (2016) Themes and developments of psychoanalytic thought in Italy. In F. Borgogno, A. Luchetti, and L. M. Coe (eds.) 2016.

Foot, J. (2015) *The Man Who Closed the Asylums. Franco Basaglia and the Revolution in Mental Health Care.* London: Verso.

França, M. O. de A. F. (2013) Foreword to Ferro. 2013.

Freud, S. ([1891] 1953) *On Aphasia*. Translated by E. Stengel. New York: International Universities Press.

———— ([1899] 1953–1964) *The Interpretation of Dreams. The Standard Edition of the Complete Psychological Works of Sigmund Freud*. Volume V. London: The Hogarth Press.

———— ([1912] 1953–1964) *Recommendations to Physicians Practising Psycho-Analyisis. The Standard Edition of the Complete Psychological Works of Sigmund Freud*. Volume XII, pp. 109–120. London: The Hogarth Press.

———— ([1917] 1953–1964) *A Difficulty in the Path of Psycho-Analysis. The Standard Edition of the Complete Psychological Works of Sigmund Freud*. Volume XV11, pp. 135–144. London: The Hogarth Press.

Gaburri, E. and Ferro, A. (1988) Gli sviluppi Kleiniani e Bion. In A. A. Semi (ed.), *Trattato di psicoanalisi*. Volume 1, pp. 289–387. Milano: Raffaello Cortina Editore.

Gibeault, A. (1991) Interpretation and transference. *Bulletin of the European Psychoanalytical Federation* 36:47–61.

Goldberg, P. (2022) Dreaming, Day-Dreaming and Sensing Things. Paper given at the Bion International Online Conference, A. Santamaria Psicoanálisis México, 12.11.2022.

———— (2023) Analytic framing and shared psychosensory experience. *Fort Da* 29:17–35.

Green, A. (2002) The crisis in psychoanalytic understanding. *Fort Da* 8:58–71.

Grinberg, L. (1957) Perturbaciones en la interpretación por la contraidentificación proyectiva. *Revista de Psicoanálisis* 14:23–30.

Grotstein, J. S. (1979) Who is the dreamer who dreams the dream and who is the dreamer who understands it – A psychoanalytic enquiry into the ultimate nature of being. *Contemporary Psychoanalysis* 15:110–169.

———— (2000) Notes on Bion's 'Memory and desire'. *Journal of the American Academy of Psychoanalysis* 28(4):687–694.

———— ([2007] 2018) *A Beam of Intense Darkness. Wilfred Bion's Legacy to Psychoanalysis*. London: Routledge.

Haddad, A. and Haddad, G. (1995) *Freud en Italie. Psychanalyse du voyage*. Paris: Albin Michel.

Harris, T. (1981) *Red Dragon*. New York: Putnam.

———— (1988) *The Silence of the Lambs*. New York: St Martin's Press.

———— (1999) *Hannibal*. New York: Delacorte Press.

Hautmann, G. (1981) My debt towards Bion: From Psychoanalysis as a theory to psycho-analysis as a mental function. *Rivista di Psicoanalisi* 27:573–586.

Hinshelwood, R. D. (2108) John Rickman behind the scenes. The influence of Lewin's field theory on practice, countertransference, and W. R. Bion. *International Journal of Psychoanalysis* 99(6):1409–1423.

———— (2023) *W. R. Bion as Clinician. Steering between Concept and Practice*. London and New York: Routledge.

Hopper, E. and Weinberg, H. (eds.) (2011) *The Social Unconscious in Persons, Groups, and Societies*. Volume 1: Mainly Theory. London: Karnac.

Huizinga, J. ([1938] 2016) *Homo Ludens. A Study of the Play-Element in Culture*. New York: Angelico Press.

IJP Open (2021) Reverie from Bion to Bionian Field Theory: Extra-analytic suggestions and clinical use. *International Journal of Psychoanalysis Open Peer Review and Debate* 8(26):1–28.

Isaacs, S. (1948) The nature and function of phantasy. In J. Rivière (ed.) 1952.

Joseph, B. (1985) Transference: The total situation. *International Journal of Psychoanalysis* 66:447–454.

Joyce, J. ([1939] 2012) *Finnegans Wake*. Ware: Wordsworth Editions.

Jung, C. G. ([1959] 2014) *The Archetypes and the Collective Unconscious. C. G. Jung, The Collected Works*. Volume 9 part 1. Translated by R. F. C. Hull. London and New York: Routledge.

Kancyper, L. (2005) The confrontation between generations as a dynamic field. In S. Lewkowicz and S. Flechner (eds.) 2005.

Kant, I. ([1784] 1970) *An Answer to the Question 'What is Enlightenment?'. Kant's Political Writings*. Edited and Introduced by H. Reiss, translation by H. B. Nisbet. Cambridge: Cambridge University Press.

Katz, W. (2013) Field of dreams: Four books by three Italians. *Contemporary Psychoanalysis* 49(3):458–483.

Keats, J. (1958) *The Letters of John Keats*, Volumes 2. Edited by H. E. Rollins. Cambridge, MA: Harvard University Press.

Kernberg O.F. (2011) Divergent contemporary trends in psychoanalytic theory. *The Psychoanalytic Review* 98(5):633–664.

Kezich, T. ([2002] 2007) *Federico Fellini. His Life and Work*. Translated by M. Proctor with V. Mazza. London and New York: I. B. Tauris.

Klein, M. ([1932] 1997) *The Psycho-Analysis of Children*. Translated by A. Strachey, revised by A. Strachey and H. A. Thorner. London: Vintage.

———— ([1961] 1998) *Narrative of a Child Analysis: The Conduct of the Psycho-Analysis of Children as Seen in the Treatment of a Ten-Year-Old Boy*. Foreword by E. Jacques. London: Vintage.

Kuhn, T. S. (1962) *The Structure of Scientific Revolutions*. Chicago, IL: University of Chicago Press.

Langs, R. (1977) Interventions in the Bipersonal Field. In R. Langs (ed.), *Technique in Transition (Classical Psychoanalysis and Its Applications)*. New York: Jason Aronson, 1977.

Leopardi, G. (2015) *Zibaldone*. Revised edition. Edited by M. Caesar and F. D'Intino, translated K. Baldwin etc. New York: Farrar, Strauss and Giroux.

Levine, H. (2021) Personal communication 18.10.2021.

———— (2022) *The Post-Bionian Field Theory of Antonino Ferro. Theoretical Analysis and Clinical Application*. London and New York: Routledge.

———— (2023) Contribution to Third Online Bion Seminar with Antonino Ferro. A. Santamaría Psicoanálisis México, 05.04.2023.

Lewin, K. (1951) *Field Theory in Social Science*. New York: Harper.

Lewkowicz, S. and Flechner, S. (eds.) ([2005] 2018) *Truth, Reality, and the Psychoanalyst. Latin American Contributions to Psychoanalysis*. Foreword by D. H. Widlöcher and C. L. Eizirik. London and New York: Routledge.

Litman, R. E. (ed.) (1966) *Psychoanalysis in the Americas*. New York: International University Press.

Maiello, S. (2012) Prenatal experiences of containment in the light of Bion's model of container/contained. *Journal of Child Psychotherapy* 38:250–267.

Matte Blanco, I. (1968) Sull'interpretazione. *Rivista di Psicoanalasi* 14:191–220.

Mazzacane, F. (2016) Some thoughts on the likely side effects of the psychoanalytical field model. *IJP Open - Open Peer Review and Debate* 3:1–27.

———— (2018) Pavia group presentation. *Revue Roumaine de Psychanalyse* 11(2):43–46.

———— (2022) The Bion-Field Theory (BFT): Theory, clinical tools, controversial points. In R. Snell R. Morgan-Jones, and D. Loewenthal (eds.) 2023.

Meltzer, D. ([1976] 1981) Temperatura e distanza come dimensioni tecniche dell'interpretazione. In D. Meltzer (ed.) *La comprensione della bellezza*, Turin: Loescher, 1981.

———— (1978) *The Kleinian Development, Part III – The Clinical Significance of the Work of Bion*. Pertshire: Clunie Press.

———— (1984) *Dream Life*. Perth: Clunie Press.

———— (1986) Riflessione sui mutamenti nel mio metodo psiconalitico. *Psicoterapia e Scienze Umane* 20:260–269.

Merleau-Ponty ([1945] 2002) *The Phenomenology of Perception*. Translated by C. Smith. London: Routledge.

——— ([1964] 1983) *L'œil et l'esprit*. Paris: Gallimard.

Milner, M. (1960) The Conception of the Body. In M. Milner (ed.) (1988), pp. 234–240.

——— (1988) *The Suppresssd Madness of Sane Men. Forty-Four Years of Exploring Psychoanalysis*. London and New York: Routledge.

Montana Katz, S. (2017) *Contemporary Psychoanalytic Field Theory. Stories, Dreams, and Metaphor*. London: Routledge.

——— Cassorla, R., and Civitarese, G. (2017) *Advances in Contemporary Psychoanalytic Field Theory. Concept and Future Development*. London: Routledge.

Morgan-Jones, R. (2010) *The Body of the Organisation and Its Health*. London: Karnac.

Neri, C. (2009) The Enlarged Notion of the Field in Psychoanalysis. In A. Ferro and R. Basile (eds.) [2009] 2018.

——— (2016) *Intervista a Claudio Neri, sul concetto di campo. A cura di Maria Giovanna Argese*. Seconda parte. Rome: Centro di Psicoanalisi Romano. https://www.youtube.com/watch?v=-uj3TUdrXGs (Consulted 08.10.2022).

——— and Selvaggi, L. (2006) Campo. In R. Barale (ed.) (2006), pp. 180–185.

Nissum Momigliano, L. (1974) Come si originano le interpretazioni nello psicoanalista. *Rivista di Psicoanalisi* 20:144–165.

——— (1984) 'Due persone che parlano in una stanza'. (Una ricerca sul dialogo analitico). *Rivista di Psicoanalisi* 30:1–17.

——— (1992) *Continuity and Change in Psychoanalysis. Letters from Milan*. London and New York: Karnac.

——— (2001) *L'ascolto rispettoso. Scritti psicoanalitici*. Milan: Raffaello Cortina.

——— and Robutti, A. (eds.) (1992) *Shared Experience. The Psychoanalytic Dialogue*. Foreword by E. Brenman. London and New York: Karnac.

Ogden, T. H. (1979) On projective identification. *International Journal of Psychoanalysis* 60:357–373.

———— (1994) The analytic third: Working with intersubjective clinical facts. *International Journal of Psychoanalysis* 75:3–19.

———— (2002) Foreword to A. Ferro. [2002] 2013.

———— (2005) *This Art of Psychoanalysis: Dreaming Undreamt Dreams and Interrupted Cries*. London: Routledge.

———— (2008) *Redisovering Psychoanalysis. Thinking and Dreaming, Learning and Forgetting*. London and New York: Routledge.

———— (2019) Ontological psychoanalysis or 'What do you want to be when you grow up?'. *The Psychoanalytic Quarterly* 88(4):661–684.

Panksepp, J. (1998) *Affective Neuroscience*. Oxford and New York: Oxford University Press.

Parsons, M. (2007) Raiding the Inarticulate. Internal setting, beyond countertransference. In M. Parsons 2013, pp. 153–168.

———— (2013) *Living Psychoanalysis. From Theory to Experience*. London and New York: Routledge.

Pavell, T. J. (1976) Possible worlds in literary semantics. *The Journal of Aesthetics and Art Criticism* 34:165–176.

Penna, C. and Hopper, E. (2022) Commentary on the special edition on developments in field theory of the *European Journal of Psychotherapy and Counselling*. Fields, systems, and silos: From electromechanics to the matrix. In R. Snell and R. Morgan-Jones 2022 and R. Snell, R. Morgan-Jones, and D. Loewnthal 2023.

Pirandello, L. ([1921] 1995) *Six Characters in Search of an Author and Other Plays*. Translated by M. Musa. London: Penguin.

Reiner, A. (2023) *W. R. Bion's Theories of Mind*. Routledge Introductions to Contemporary Psychoanalysis. London and New York: Routledge.

Renik, O. (2002) Introduction to Ferro [1996] 2013.

Riolo, F. (1983) Sogno e teoria della conoscenza in psicoanalisi. *Rivista di Psicoanalisi* 29:279295.

Rivière, J. (1952) (ed.) *Developments in Psychoanalysis*. London: Hogarth Press.

Roos, K. (2020) Review of A. Ferro and L. Nicoli, *The New Analyst's Guide to the Galaxy: Questions about Contemporary Psychoanalysis* (2017) 2018. *International Journal of Psychoanalysis* 101:849–853.

Rorty, R. (1989) *Contingency, Irony, and Solidarity*. Cambridge: Cambridge University Press.

Sabbadini, A. and Ferro, A. (2010) Review of M. and W. Baranger 2009. *International Journal of Psychoanalysis* 91:415–429.

Sigourny Award (2007) Antonino Ferro, MD, 2007. https://www.sigourneyaward.org/recipientlist/2019/1/28/antonino-ferro-md-2007. (Consulted 03.01.23).

Snell, R. (2021) *Cézanne and the Post-Bionian Field. An Exploration and a Meditation*. London: Routledge.

———— and Morgan-Jones, R. (eds.) (March 2022) *Developments in Field Theory*. Special Issue of the *European Journal of Psychotherapy and Counselling* 24(1). London: Routledge.

Morgan-Jones, R. and Loewenthal, D. (eds.) (2023) *Developments in Field Theory for Psychotherapists, Psychoanalysts and Counsellors*. London: Routledge.

Spillius, E. B. (ed.) (1988) *Melanie Klein Today. Developments in Theory and Practice. Volume 2: Mainly Practice*. London and New York: Routledge.

Vermote, R. (2019) *Reading Bion*. London and New York: Routledge.

Wilde, O. F. O. W. ([1891] 2010) *The Decay of Lying and Other Essays*. London: Penguin.

Williams, R. ([1961] 2013) *The Long Revolution*. Cardigan: Parthian.

Winnicott, D. W. (1960) The Theory of the Parent-Infant Relationship. In D. W. Winnicott (ed.) ([1965] 1990), pp. 37–55.

———— ([1965] 1990) *The Maturational Process and the Facilitating Environment*. London: Karnac.

—— ([1971] 1985) *Playing and Reality*. London: Penguin Books.

—— (1974) Fear of Breakdown. *International Journal of Psychoanalysis* 1:103–107.

Young, J. Z. ([1950] 1956) *Doubt and Certainty in Science. A Biologist's Reflections on the Brain*. Reprint edition. Oxford: Oxford University Press.

Index

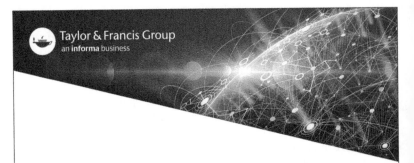

For Product Safety Concerns and Information please contact our EU representative GPSR@taylorandfrancis.com Taylor & Francis Verlag GmbH, Kaufingerstraße 24, 80331 München, Germany

Printed and bound by CPI Group (UK) Ltd, Croydon, CR0 4YY
08/06/2025
01897002-0001